# CHARLESTON

# Salt *and* Iron

## The beauty, strength and timeless allure of the South's crown jewel

Foreword by Mary Alice Monroe

*New York Times Best Selling Author*
*The Beach House Trilogy and*
*The Lowcountry Summer Trilogy*

Edited by
Wendy Nilsen Pollitzer

**LI**
**LTD**

Lydia Inglett Ltd. Publishing
*Award-winning publishers of elegant books*

# Contents

Curls and Windows. Photo by Sandy Dimke

This book is dedicated to my mother, Shirley Nilsen.
You told me to face life head-on, with determination and
without fear. You taught me to listen with an authentic ear
and speak with a confident voice.
Most of all, you taught me the true meaning of love.
You are my hero and best friend, and I'll always be your baby.
– WENDY NILSEN POLLITZER

## Charleston Salt and Iron™

*The beauty, strength and timeless
allure of the South's crown jewel*

Edited by Wendy Nilsen Politzer

ISBN: 978-1-938417-27-6

Second book in the Impressions
of Our America Book Series™

Front Cover: Winter Facade by Sandy Dimke

Published by Lydia Inglett Ltd. Publishing
www.lydiainglett.com
www.starbooks.biz
301 Central Ave. #181
Hilton Head Island, SC 29926
info@starbooks.biz

To order more copies of this or any
of our award-winning books,
visit our on-line bookstore:

# www.STARBOOKS.biz
The place for beautiful, thoughtful gift books

*Net casting with Jack Russell. Photo by Michelle Bolton*

"There are no strangers here, only
family and friends who haven't yet met."

- HANK FUTCH
Bassist, founding member, Blue Dogs

*The Rutledge House, located at 116 Broad Street, was built circa 1763 by John Rutledge, a governor and president of South Carolina during the Revolution. In 1902, Mayor Robert Goodwyn Rhett purchased the home. Rhett's butler, William Deas, invented and served She-crab soup to one of the home's regular guests, President William Howard Taft. The intricate ironwork was added in 1853. Photo by Martha Lawrence*

# Foreword

Charleston is rich in its sense of place. We need only look to her expansive history to appreciate the role she played in the foundation of our great nation. From the seventeenth and eighteenth centuries, our port has seen countless newcomers—some willing, others not. It is estimated that 60 to 80% of African American citizens can trace at least one ancestor back to Charleston, South Carolina. With the wisdom of retrospect, we witness how two social strata—the great cotton and rice plantations and the African slaves—came together over the course of time to form many of the Lowcountry's most treasured cultural traditions. We celebrate the unique Gullah-Geechee culture that has survived in our barrier islands. And in each era, the South's historic crown jewel, Charleston has glittered as a beacon of sophistication, culture, and tradition for generations.

The landscape is our common ground. From the pounding surf and the swift tidal currents to the majestic lakes and verdant countryside. From the scents of freshly tilled soil, jasmine and pluff mud, to the sight of countless fireflies lighting up the dirt roads, moss dripping like ragged lace from the drooping boughs of ancient oaks, elegant verandas, rocking chairs on front porches, wood cabins deep in the forests and cobblestone streets in the city, to the sounds of swelling cicadas on summer nights, the piercing cries of ospreys, hawks and eagles and the omnipresent high hum of mosquitoes—these are hallmarks of our Southern home.

Yet as dramatic and influential as these broad strokes of Charleston's landscape may be to help us define that elusive sense of place, it is in the personal stories that we explore the poignant, heartwarming experiences that define life in the Holy City. The words of the locals sweep away the fairytale and reveal the true, every day human experience.

In this collection of essays, some of Charleston's most beloved citizens share what it means to live in this land carved of marsh and sea. To work here, raise a family here, grow old here. Some authors may claim ties to a historic family with a long pedigree. Others are newcomers, those "from off" who have traveled to our states and now call them home. These individual stories of inspiration, motivation, joy and sorrow, discovery and loss, failure and triumph collectively are our Songs of the South—our Charleston.

2015 was a year of challenges for Charleston. As I write, we are battling the unprecedented, historic rainfall that has flooded the state and will leave many of our citizens homeless. In her long history, Charleston has weathered war, hunger, disease, economic depression, hurricanes, and floods. Our city has triumphed over adversity time and again. I know that in aftermath of this flooding, too, neighbor will help neighbor. Only a few months earlier we endured the brutal slaying of innocents at "Mother Emanuel," the oldest African Methodist Episcopal church in the Southern United States. Perhaps Charleston's shining moment came when she revealed to the world a lesson in forgiveness and community bonds and moving forward undivided.

**Mary Alice Monroe**
*New York Times* Best Selling Author of *The Beach House Trilogy* and *The Lowcountry Summer Trilogy*

Photo by Mic Smith

*Botany Bay Road. Photo by Kelley Luikey*

*Boone Hall Plantation. Photo by Eric Horan*

# Introduction

I wasn't born into a lineage of a recognized family name, and still, I've always considered myself to be a daughter of Charleston. She cradled me at birth at Roper Hospital and gave me a coveted distinction—to be born and raised as one of her children.

As with all of my brothers and sisters, she led me down a diverse path. Through cobblestone alleys, avenues of oaks, old country roads, sandy beaches, pluff mud trails and a sundry of bridges, she guided me to embrace unity among our differences and solidarity as "one Charleston." She taught me life-long lessons of coastal stewardship through the ebb and flow of her estuaries. She gave me an international appreciation of art and music. She taught me to respect her buildings, her waterways, her culture, her cuisine, her past, her future, and above all, her people.

Even today, Charleston does all of this effortlessly, with no fuss and no bother, yet progresses with elegant composure and distinguished grace. She wears flip flops and white gloves, eats shrimp off a newspaper and respectfully replies. Amidst a coastal playground of winding creeks and pristine beaches, the peninsula within her mighty harbor gently reminds us of her history and enduring strength. She is my salt, and she is my iron.

*Charleston Salt and Iron* is a compilation of sentiments that collectively pronounce and illustrate Charleston's beauty, strength and timeless allure as the South's crown jewel. Through reflective words and images, contributors embrace their love of the Holy City by offering personal stories, memories and creative testimony. They are people who have made differences in our community, and, in my opinion, representatives of true Southern charm.

I credit the integrity of *Charleston Salt and Iron* to all of the authors, photographers and poets who graciously submitted their eloquent words and defining images that reflect a true sense of living in Charleston.

In addition to all of the contributors and photographers who respectfully shared their compositions and their time, I would like to thank, in no particular order, Marlene Navor, Richard Weedman, Monica Tanouye, Angela May, Susan Lucas, Jennifer Wallace, Marcy Krawcheck,

Jennifer Scott, Fran Zeuli, Katia Jenkins Thomas, Emily Gildea, Angela Wicke, www.lowcountryloveletters.com, Kristin Wolfe, Mary Roberts, Chad Shores, Andrea Gay Leary, Caroline Porter, Coastal Community Foundation, Spoleto Festival USA, Southeastern Wildlife Exposition, The Charleston RiverDogs, The Cooper River Bridge Run, The Citadel and College of Charleston.

Additionally, I extend my gratitude to Mary Alice Monroe who accepted the challenging task of writing *Charleston Salt and Iron's* foreword. I am truly honored, to have you, one of my literary heroes and mentors, write this for me Mary Alice. Thank you. And to my publisher, Lydia Inglett, here's to our second book together.

I can't begin to thank all of the wonderful people who have walked with me on this journey we call life. To all of my friends and family from Clemson, Anderson, Beaufort, Mount Pleasant and Charleston, I give big hugs and blown kisses your way. You know who you are.

To my immediate family, especially my mom and dad, Shirley and Stewart Nilsen, thank you for giving me the memories of a secure, carefree childhood. You gave me my best asset, my set of values. I love you.

And finally, I want to thank my angels, my two daughters, Abbie and Julia. There just aren't words to describe my love for you. Both of you will always be my inspiration and the truest role models for a simple, faith-filled life. I'll always be your proud Mama first before anything else on this journey.

To Charleston, the greatest city in the world!

**Wendy Nilsen Pollitzer**
Author, *SOUTH, What it Means to be Here in Heart or in Spirit,*
*Images of America: Isle of Palms* and *Images of America: Port Royal*

Photo by Paul Nurnberg

*Charleston Market at Night. Photo by Steven Hyatt*

*View from St. Michael's. Photo by Steven Hyatt*

# The Jewel Still Shines

If you travel, you've had this conversation a hundred times.

"Where are you from?"

"I'm from Charleston."

"South Carolina?"

"Of course, is there another one?"

That's when the swoon begins, and the person you're talking to in the airport or in a meeting far from home goes, "Oh, I just love Charleston. It's so beautiful, I can't believe you actually live there!"

From that moment on, you are a person of interest. Not because you're rich or famous or powerful, but because you live in this paradise that has been lauded worldwide for its beauty, history, culinary excellence, art, friendliness, and its gentle climate.

In the company of strangers, you stand out among those who toil away in other nondescript places where a new McDonald's or the repaving of the by-pass is the talk of the town.

By last count there are a million places in the United States that look exactly alike. But Charleston is not among them. It is a jewel in America's crown, a jewel that survived the Revolution, the Civil War, and reconstruction, as well as many self-inflicted wounds that brought her to her knees.

Thus the attitude I speak of, the one that makes this old town special, comes from the strand in our Southern DNA that stood up against the British and was trampled by the Union Army, only to rise from the ashes of anger and indignity to tell the rest of the country that Charleston is a survivor.

*Off of Broad. Photo by Marge Agin*

As a Charlestonian, I smile when my distinct accent catches the ear of people from "off." When my seersucker suit announces my presence and perspective on life. When people are taken aback by my humble manners and genuine concern for others.

For to live here is more than geographical luck. It is the gift of a lifetime that keeps on giving until you join those in the city's old graveyards and become an eternal link between the past and future.

Knowing this makes you special, confident, and above all, envied.

This is why nobody leaves Charleston unless ordered to. And even then they drop a small anchor in a brackish creek or tie a lifeline around a majestic oak, because they know they're going to find their way back someday.

---

**Ken Burger,** 1949-2015. In Memoriam. Author, *Swallow Savannah, Sister Santee, Salkehatchie Soup,* and *Baptized in Sweet Tea. The Post and Courier* sports columnist, 1984 to 2011. *"Miss our friend, celebrate his impact."*

The gardens of the Unitarian Church at 4 Archdale Street connect Meeting Street to King Street and walkways through the Charleston Library Society yard and the courtyard of the Gibbes Museum of Art.

The nostalgic landmark on King Street, Tellis Pharmacy, closed its doors in 2012.

The Governor's House Inn, 117 Broad Street. Former residence of Governor Edward Rutledge, the youngest signer of the Declaration of Independence.

The Thomas Rose House, 59 Church Street. Constructed circa 1735, it is considered one of Charleston's best preserved colonial dwellings.

"Listen as you walk her streets—you hear the people, the sounds of everyday life, and something more ...

It's the voices of those who came before us, down through history, who built this place.

Today, we add our voices to the chorus."

*The William Harvey House, circa 1770, 58 Meeting Street. The western half of a double tenement (eighteenth century term denoting rental property) built by Harvey. John H. Doscher purchased the dwelling in 1872 and altered the ground floor into a grocery store with a Meeting Street commercial storefront. Grocer Peter C. Christantou purchased the building in 1917 and operated "Pete's," a popular neighborhood grocery store for the next 60 years. In 1982 the property was returned to its historic use as a private residence.*

*Charlestonians take great pride in the value of generous reception. Cordial hosts welcome their guests with first impressions of gas lanterns, grand porches and intimate gardens to offer comfort and a warm embrace.*

# Beneath the Cleansing Flood

She was my first love, and as a child I thought of her as perfect in every way.

Bicycles and skateboards lay askew on her sidewalks, patiently awaiting the return of their jockeys. Family dogs snoozed in the center of Meeting Street, basking in the sunshine that slipped between the oaks. Mr. Wagoner guided the city's lone carriage, and left in his wake the somehow pleasant aroma of pastures. Backyard Christmas tree forts popped up in early January, and young warriors staged commando raids on enemy encampments. Hazel Parker ruled the East Bay Playground with a velvet hammer, while Henry Lowndes coached three seasons of sports.

The Isle of Palms was known not for beaches, but for bingo under the roar of industrial fans. Grandmothers called grandmothers to secure dancing school partners for their one-day-old grandchildren. Backyard mountaineers climbed ivy-covered walls to see how far they could travel without touching the ground. Palmetto trees at the Battery served as sidelines when Mr. Barkley quarterbacked pick-up football games. Pete's Candy Store boasted glass jars of heaven for those with a dime. Box's at King and Tradd provided free air for pressure-starved bike tires. The Market was empty, save for when it hosted weekend flea markets. Plaster dust lay unswept on the floors of East Bay mansions.

Birthday cake at Skateland felt bigger than Disney. Dirt roads paved Kiawah, and a jungle ruled the end of Isle of Palms. Friends met for dove hunts without membership dues. Burbage's charge accounts and bike delivery seemed as natural as air. Low-hanging Japanese plums offered after-school candy. Oysters were steamed using sheet metal and crocus sacks. Boys with empty pockets searched Broad Street's sidewalk grates for change. …

I thought she was perfect in every way.

Charleston was my home. Then, the world discovered her. Once a lady wearing flip-flops and shorts with her hair in a ponytail, now she is a packaged and proper superstar—with expertly applied makeup, designer gowns, and the finest Italian shoes. She is an international diva, with the world at her feet.

Glossy magazines fawn over her dining, comparing her to such culinary meccas as New Orleans, San Francisco and New York. Her shopping is legendary— where once stood local boutiques, King Street now boasts national chains rivaling Chicago's Miracle Mile. The tourism industry booms, providing jobs and wealth and opportunities for businesses of all types and sizes. The College of Charleston evolved into an elite and expensive university, attracting students from throughout the nation. Even industry has rediscovered the Lowcountry, as evidenced by the recent arrival of world-class manufacturers.

Most say she is far more beautiful today: Renovated and restored homes; fine arts and world-renowned festivals; things to see and do every day of the year; a growing economy with cranes in the skylines; even cruise ships slip through her bustling harbors to deliver visitors to her shore. Her arms are open, welcoming all who come to live, work, and play.

Who am I to question her changes? I played a part in them. I carried her to the altar of money, and bled her for my share. Why wouldn't I? People, places, eras … they all change. And the changes I helped bring about are wonderful—who can object to such engrossing distractions? Golf! Nightlife! Tours! Spas! Baby Gap! Spoleto! Increases in property value!

But … sometimes I wonder. About myself.

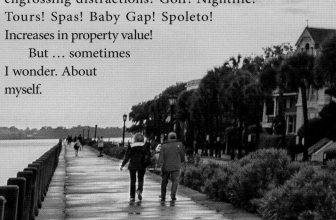

About my role. And I think about Charleston's overwhelming yet cleansing floods.

You see, for all my life downtown Charleston has flooded. If there's a high tide and a heavy downpour, most of the city is a creek—in some places a river. I tell myself the floods are an unstoppable force, impossible to combat. I tell myself nothing can be done, because resisting the nature of things is futile. I tell myself the floods aren't actually bad, because they sweep the streets clean.

But still, I think about my decisions and my former home—as I watch the floodwater and dirt and unsightly things carried by gravity to the harbor, where they are absorbed and vanish, swept out to sea with the tide.

**Prioleau Alexander**
Author, *You Want Fries With That?*

*East Battery, Sunset. Photo by Jonathan Jackson*

# A Great Love Affair

There is a timeworn joke, which asks the question, "How many Charlestonians does it take to change a light bulb?" We are told that it takes five: two to hold the ladder, one to summon the servant to screw in the bulb, one to mix the Martinis, and one to reminisce on how light bulbs ain't what they used to be.

No one has been ever lukewarm about Charleston. People either love it or hate it, usually for purely personal reasons, and with opinions justified with the tenacity of religious conviction. Under the ever-vigilant eye of a watchful citizenry, the city's bricks, mortar, and character have been defended against unseemly alteration. What has come down to us today are people-scale streetscapes, a citywide comfort zone devoid of most of the shattering exuberances of Modernism.

A learned scholar once observed that Charlestonians' compelling sense of stewardship derives from one of the most distinguishing characteristics of Lowcountry folks: the importance of their personal connection with a particular place or community to their identities. This deeply felt sense of place is marked by an intuitive feeling of continuity, of having roots, a stake hold on the land, which transcends mere ownership or sentimentality.

I like to tell people who ask that I wasn't born here, but I got here as soon as I could. On my arrival in 1961, I was a teenager just entering The Military College of South Carolina. On those rare weekend days when cadets were released to pass through the iron gates and enter the realm of polite society, I made it my mission to explore every inch of downtown Charleston. It was unlike any place I had ever seen, having led a mostly sheltered childhood in the rural sandhills of the South Carolina midlands, and, of course, I took advantage of

Photo by Martha Lawrence

every last minute of my all-too-brief respite from military rigors.

To me Charleston was an exotic and magical place. The residents here were inclined to be kind and generous to uniformed cadets, for many had experienced cadet life, too. On one occasion I was invited in off the sidewalk to have sherry at a delightful gathering of downtown dowagers. I still remember savoring the heavy, perfumed air while walking about in the evenings and early mornings, and being impressed with the long views of the sparkling, wide waters of the rivers, which ebbed and flowed at Charleston's borders. I was continually amazed to discover the curious details of a seemingly unending array of centuries-old architecture.

I was totally smitten with the beauty, sophistication and pleasant nature of Charleston's young ladies, one of whom I married about fifty years ago. Charleston was and is the perfect place in which to fall in love and make a home. There is a little more going on now—more people, more traffic, more noise. It is a combination that is a little messier than it was fifty-five years ago … but I like it.

**Ben Moise**
Author, *Ramblings of a Lowcountry Game Warden* and Conservation Officer with the South Caolina Department of Natural Resources (Ret.)

*Hibernian Hall, 105 Meeting Street, is a historic meeting hall and social venue. Built in 1840 by Thomas Ustick Walter, it is a fine example of Greek Revival architecture. In 1860 the Charleston Convention was held here, and the Democratic party failed to select a presidential nominee due to divided opinion on slavery ensuring victory for the Republicans. Photo by Martha Lawrence*

*Market Street. Photo by Charles Merry*

# A Memory in My Eyes

My old diesel truck tunneled through the canopy of live oak branches of Stocks Creek Road. We were making our way to our old family place in the heart of the ACE basin to celebrate Thanksgiving with family and friends. My wife Caroline was beside me. My oldest son, Connor, was in the back seat of the 4-door truck, keeping watch over casseroles and Mac 'n Cheese.

As we rambled around the dirt curve, the oak canopy surrendered to the marsh grass that lines Stocks Creek. We spotted something large and black about a hundred yards distant; and as we drew nearer, we realized that, gathered on the small bridge, was a flock of Turkey Vultures, or as we call them in the Lowcountry, "buzzards." "Probably a deer carcass," I said to my wife. One by one the buzzards took to the air. Now, only a single brave bird was standing on the carcass. When we were about 100 feet away, the final bird beat its wings into flight, leaving its Thanksgiving feast unattended.

Suddenly, the "dead" animal stood up! A young black lab mix, barely out of the puppy stage, stood wagging his tail and smiling the "doggy smile" as I stopped the truck. We weren't exactly sure what to do with him, but we knew we couldn't leave him there. I opened the back door, and with a little effort, managed to coax the skinny pup into the truck.

We drove the final few miles to our place, and by the time the turkey was served, our new dog had a name, Buzzard.

Buzzard wasn't much for adventure. Skittish and scared of his own shadow, he mistrusted everything. Gun shy of course, and afraid of water, he would patiently wait as we walked down the dock to the boat. And he would be standing in the same spot to greet us many hours later, tail wagging, after a fishing trip or a boat ride to Edisto.

Buzzy loved people, but didn't care much for other dogs. I often speculated that he must have run with a pack of dogs who probably hunted together, and thus competed for food. I remember the day that an unfortunate coon dog, GPS collar and all, wandered up to the house. Buzzy took after him like hell unleashed, expertly tripping him by biting his hind legs, and going for the throat when he was down. If I hadn't been there to stop him, the coon dog would surely have been killed. He was a great hunter. My friends would watch, with bust-a-gut laughter when he herded entire packs of armadillo, leaping around them like a deer, until he plucked out the fattest one for his meal. We would always stop him before he ate them … at least the ones we caught him with.

Besides being a hunter, Buzzy didn't do very much. At our home on the Isle of Palms, he was just out of place. He was the only dog on the island who was unable to walk on the beach without a leash, because of his constant urge to fight with other dogs. After several embarrassing run-ins with island dogs and their owners, we decided to face the facts. You could take Buzzard out of the country, but you could never take the country out of Buzzard. He would forever after remain leashed for beach walks.

Early on, my wife had a strong dislike for Buz. He just couldn't do anything right. His distrust of just about everything was to his own detriment, and everyday activities like jumping in the car sometimes became major events, like the time he pulled away from his collar at the pet hotel and ran into traffic on Highway 17, cars skidding and almost hitting him.

Then one early summer night out in the country, Buzzard became a hero.

I was relaxing on the front porch, strumming my guitar in the dark. The only other audible sound was the gentle rush of water against the dock pilings of the outgoing tide. Buzzard was lying on the floor at my feet, occasionally lifting his ears to detect far-off movements of animals in the woods. A sound at the edge of the woods brought Buzzard to full alert, and he bounded down the stairs. I didn't give his behavior much thought, as this was a regular occurrence for Buz. He was a country dog, and these were his woods. He hit the ground in full run toward the tree line, barking and closing the distance on whatever he heard in an instant. The second he reached the woods, there was a loud "BOOM," the piercing crack of a high-powered rifle assaulted the soft strains of music, water and crickets. I leaped from my rocking chair and bolted for the safety of the house. This was not deer season. Far from it. In fact it wasn't any season. I had no gun for protection. Being gun shy, Buzzard flew back to the relative safety of the porch. I grabbed my keys and belted, "come on Buz" and ran for my truck. I opened the door and Buzzard leapt in. I floored the big diesel, tires spewing dirt heading for the tree line. I ran the truck completely into the woods where the shot had rang out. A big, loud truck barreling through the woods can be an intimidating weapon. I hit the brakes just in time to stop before crashing into a tree, reversed, and backed out of there. I spun the truck around and headed out of the property.

Who was wandering around in our woods with a high-powered rifle? Was it a poacher? How did he get so far into private property? Why was he there? How long had he been watching me? There will never be any definitive answers to these questions. The reason he fired his rifle though, was probably to stop a 90-pound black dog from possibly attacking him.

Years have passed since that June night, with no other similar occurrence before or since. Buzzard went patiently about his task of muzzling his way into my family's hearts, his shiny black snout now flecked with gray. I watched out of the kitchen window undetected, as my wife, tending her garden, would stop to talk to Ol' Buz and give him a hug. After years of being afraid to walk down the dock, he finally found the courage to hop on my big Carolina Skiff. He would stand on the bow surrounded by children, as we slid towards Edisto, jumping off at sand bars to wade in the muddy water as the kids swam and frolicked.

As the years passed, Buz developed hip problems. He still had the heart of a hunter, but had problems walking. I would talk softly to him as he lay on the weathered porch, his brown, soulful eyes searching the woods for movement.

The day Buzzard passed was uneventful. I wrapped him in a blanket and lay him in the bed of my truck. I drove slowly to our country house, and placed him in the resting place that I had prepared for him overlooking the Cheehaw River.

It's difficult to explain how an old mutt can work his way into a family's hearts so completely. All that I know is that he is greatly missed. There is a void in our trips to the country now, without Buzzard's presence.

Shortly after his passing I wrote him a song, as much to make me feel better as anything else.

*Buzzard close your eyes now, it's time to go to sleep*
*Daddy's got something in his eyes, must be a memory*
*I raised you from a puppy, healthy, strong and fat*
*How long ago in dog years was that?*

CHORUS:
*Dog is just God spelled backwards*
*Yes we loved you so, as a matter of factwards*
*I'll leave your favorite bone on the old duck pond road*
*To make sure you find your way home*

---

**Clay Rice**
Silhouette Artist and Author, *The Stick, Mama Let's Make a Moon, The Lonely Shadow* and *Ants 'N Uncles*

Photo by Mic Smith

# Past, Present and Into the Future

As I reflect on the beat and the rhythm and the soundtrack of my life, it is my beloved hometown of Charleston that is the essence and the core of the tunes that play in my heart and my head. As a sixth generation Charlestonian, describing who I am or what I wanted from life and how I was going to define success is a chorus of my upbringing, most clearly heard through those who came before me. From this legacy I am many things. I am a Southern, Jewish, philanthropist, mother, volunteer, friend, business owner, and waterway loving-woman.

What I love most about Charleston today is the vibrancy that is creating our future while celebrating our deep past. It is not the success that came before me but the success I will make during my lifetime. It's about the people I've known my whole life and the people coming here I have yet to meet. It's the conflicted memories of social, religious, and racial injustices and school integration tempered by the social diversity I love today. It's the foods I grew up on and the inspired scents, smells and, tastes in the Lowcountry today. It's the languid scene of seersucker-suited lawyers and the energy of the digital, creative, aeronautics, medical, and educational talent propelling Charleston forward. It's knowing there are many in Charleston who struggle with needs to be met and the outpouring of generosity by Lowcountry Giving Day contributors.

About six years ago I returned to live the rest of my life in Charleston after more than a decade living in Utah. I made a decision to return to the neighborhood I grew up in and renovated a home on a tidal creek. The sound of *Isn't it Nice To be Home Again* resonates as I wave and reconnect to multiple generations of neighborhood people who are still here and to the energy of the young who experience this peaceful neighborhood's renaissance as my young friends did generations ago.

I am the oldest of two daughters. My parents met and married one year after meeting at college in Louisiana. My sister Jan and I were raised by a beautiful, fun, energetic and welcoming mother who loved having scores of Charleston kids hang out on our dock—the only dock on Wappoo Creek at the time. I still run into people who know me because they hung out on the Pearlstine's dock. My father became and remains a Charleston legend for his business success, philanthropic deeds and most certainly because of his "broke the mold" personality. He will always be The Budman. He was a great beer man, and I aspired to follow in his footsteps.

I graduated college to the tune of *I Am Woman Hear Me Roar*, although as a woman in the beer and alcohol business it often felt like I was bumping my head on the proverbial glass ceiling rather than breaking through it. It was not an easy time. One time smack in the middle of a business conversation, an Anheuser-

*Be Still. Photo by Paul Andrew Dunker*

Busch VP stopped to comment that he couldn't believe I was pregnant again. He was a VP during the time I couldn't be "approved" by his company to run our family business. My father hated the pressure, and he must have thought how much easier it would've been if I had been a boy.

A couple of years ago I managed the sale of our fifth generation business established in 1862 when an unsolicited offer was presented to us. It was a tough decision. We loved our employees and called them our family. In a business sense it was a good offer, and we accepted it. The first thing I did was give a lot of my part of the proceeds away. My family lives by my grandmother's saying: "Service is the price you pay for the rewards you reap." Over the generations, my family has contributed to many of Charleston's initiatives and organizations. I am very proud that I have been able to establish at MUSC the Susan Pearlstine Sarcoidosis Center of Excellence with a mission to "improve the lives of Sarcoidosis patients and their families."

Charleston and I have a lot to celebrate and a lot more to do. I serve as a board member at various organizations and worked to organize my neighborhood association. Recently the second of my three kids settled in Charleston. And most exciting of all, I have formed a new business, and I plan to develop a new waterfront venue on the Ashley River which will be enjoyed by many generations after me.

Last year I wanted to attend a lunch meeting that my father organized. To my surprise I was told it was a "father and son" group. I went anyway. Me and 99 guys. My father welcomed everyone, then mentioned my presence there. He said "Susan said she was coming because it's the year 2015 in Charleston, South Carolina and not Saudi Arabia." Then he paused and said, "I think she's probably right." When clearly the Charleston of my past meets the Charleston present. And my heart sings . . .

**Susan Pearlstine**
Founder of The Pearlstine Company and
Former Owner/Director Pearlstine Distributors

Photo by Jack Alterman

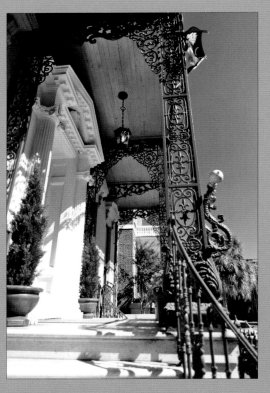

Antiquated and weathered, contemporary and new, Charleston's iron work is a metaphor for strength—not just of gates, railings and buildings, but of her people—hard wrought and persevering.

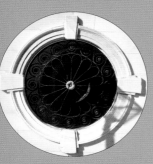

*Photos by Martha Lawrence*

# Bin Yahs, Come Yahs and Connectedness

Charleston makes sense to me. She's the matriarch of the Lowcountry family who gave birth both to the people and to the towns that are all related to her and that define her character and her personality, her past, present, and future.

Charleston is the hub from which all of our nearby towns grew. These communities are connected to her by roads and often water. It's hard for me to think of Charleston without thinking of McClellanville's fishing fleet, Summerville as a retreat from the big city, and the flow of Mount Pleasant's Shem Creek and Wando River.

Created by trade and travel, those original roadway and waterway connections may now be secondary to why we are family, but we still maintain a psychic bond that ties our communities together. This organic connectedness helps every town and neighborhood, every marsh and river, fit into a whole, each part of which has its own "wow" factor.

And the people of greater Charleston are as unique as the places. We're all related—some as eccentric aunts and uncles, some as grandparents passing down tradition, and some as offspring bucking for change. Some are successful, some not so much. Some revel in the city, some escape to the country. For some it's débutante balls; for others, it's the Pour House.

When I came to Charleston in 1979, people told me, "Lots of luck because that town doesn't like outsiders." Maybe my experience would have been different 75 years ago, but from the start, the people and places here have been consistently welcoming and friendly.

I've experienced this with every person who calls, emails, or walks in the door at Coastal Community Foundation, my daytime home on the Charleston peninsula. Some of these people are "Bin Yah," having lived in Charleston for generations, and others are "Come Yah," drawn by a magnetic attraction to everything this place has to offer. The Bin Yahs appreciate the generosity of money and fresh perspectives that new folks bring to Charleston. Come Yahs are drawn to Charleston by her character, traditions and beauty, created by the old guard. They help to foster change while honoring Charleston's spirit and soul, and the Bin Yahs respect them for it.

At the Foundation, our mission is to foster philanthropy for the lasting good of the community. We bring people together from all walks of life, all hometowns and all beliefs, and help to assure continuity and change—continuity of what is precious and change to move forward.

I've met with thousands of donors and nonprofits in my time at the Foundation and they are all united in their positivity. When you get the right combination of laser-focused commitment, timing and people in a room, meaningful change happens. It's how we got One80 Place and the Center for Heirs' Property Preservation. It's how we got Lowcountry Food Bank and bus shelters at CARTA stops. It's how we'll see a lot more change in generations to come, while always remaining vigilant to maintain what defines this community.

Some people say they don't give to charity, because they don't support handouts. Those same people enjoy a beautiful drive to work every day on a road shaded by oak trees that their local land trust preserved. They come home to a Golden Retriever rescued by the nonprofit animal shelter. On Saturdays, these same people

"*All of our lives are enriched by the nonprofit sector in ways we don't think about or even realize. We can't right the wrongs in our community overnight, but I've seen nonprofits change tens of thousands of lives for the better.*"

*St. Michael's from Broad Street. Photo by Steven Hyatt*

buy local produce from a farmers market, which was subsidized by a nonprofit food hub. They dress for an evening performance of theatre or music thinking that buying their ticket provides their fair share, when in actuality, the performance wouldn't have happened without charitable donations to supplement the cost of those tickets.

All of our lives are enriched by the nonprofit sector in ways we don't think about or even realize. We can't right the wrongs in our community overnight, but I've seen nonprofits change tens of thousands of lives for the better. And whether they're a Come Yah or a Bin Yah, the donors I've worked with for decades strengthen those same nonprofits every day, joining them to make an impact. That's really how philanthropy works best—when we come together for a focused common cause and remember that everyone is at the table because they want to make something positive happen.

So why have I stayed here after all these years? Because whether or not it's a realistic reflection of the rest of the world, Charleston is positivity, generosity, continuity and change. And that's the kind of place I want to call home.

**By Richard Hendry**
Program Officer for Coastal Community Foundation since 1983

Photo by Adam Chandler

*East Bay and Battery. Photo by Steven Hyatt*

# Sharing the History

Charleston, the grand lady that she is, possesses many fine attributes. She expresses ageless beauty. She is enduring and endearing. She is a home to many and a haven for countless others. She embodies grace, strength and an endless depth of character. Her story touches on every sense and emotion. A native's basic and natural existence, a wilderness adventure, a settler's hope, a colonist's opportunity, a pirate's crowned jewel, a religious and educational cornerstone, a military strategist's conquest, and nature's target. Charleston has endured and produced generations of a people who have lived, adapted, and progressed under a wide spectrum of physical, social, and economic trials and experiences. All of this has produced what is referred to as the "Charlestonian." She is grand indeed, and her beauty is a reflection of those who love and respect her and call her home.

The home where I grew up is unique. My father found this old brick house on an acre of land full of live oaks, dogwoods, camellias, azaleas, and Spanish moss. The house was built in 1926 by a family that had once owned two different Lowcountry plantations. The builders brought pieces of their past, old Charleston brick, heart pine floors, multiple fireplaces, wrought iron, and millstones into the home. My mother was not as enthusiastic about the prospect of this becoming her place of residence, because it had been vacant for some time. My mother saw one thing: a lifelong project. Dad viewed the issues as temporary obstacles: lipstick and rouge, if you will, and he bought that old house without mother's blessing. They adapted and worked hard for many years to make it a loving and happy home, a home where we enjoyed many birthday parties, neighborhood picnics, pig pickin's, graduations, Easter egg hunts, and lazy summer days under the shade of those old oak trees. Today, that home has been fully renovated. Part of the lot has been sold, and the landscaping has changed. The old Blue Heron that used to perch in one of the live oaks in the backyard is long gone. There are no more baseball games or marathon sessions of "roll the bat" in that side yard, where a Charleston single house now stands. We found the original builder's blueprints, which are now elegantly displayed in the back hallway for visitors to enjoy. But I will forever have memories of my mother collecting pink, white, and candy striped camellias from the yard in her large sweetgrass basket, and bringing them inside to arrange on our dining room table or to prepare for me to take to a shut-in neighbor to enjoy. That property screams Charleston and the Lowcountry to me. Strong, and full of character, love, timeless beauty, history, vision, and progress.

Charleston is where I was born and where I will spend my life. She has sheltered me, educated me and molded me. As an author, I strive for excellence in my craft. My hope and prayer is that my writing will inspire each reader. There are three components that I work to incorporate into my writing: a brief history lesson, a detailed account of an event and a takeaway or educational portion. Charleston has taught me this. Charleston has taught me to protect and honor history, as it is sacred indeed. She has taught me to enjoy life, as she has so much to offer in and around her beautiful landscape. I have also learned that if I do not share these experiences with others, and encourage them to do the same, that her beauty and character will fade and become just another torn page in a dusty history book.

---

**Michael M. Cochran**
Avid outdoorsman, writer and location manager
Glasspro, Inc.

Photo by Ashley James Photography

*"Charleston has taught me to protect and honor history, as it is sacred indeed. She has taught me to enjoy life, as she has so much to offer in and around her beautiful landscape."*

Photos by Martha Lawrence.

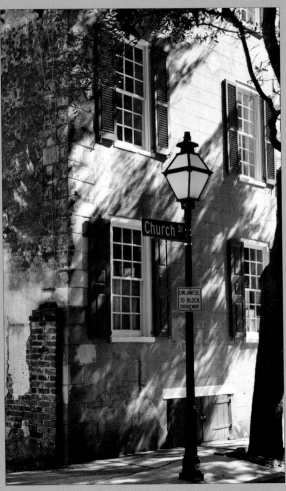

*"I have also learned that if I do not share these experiences with others, and encourage them to do the same, that her beauty and character will fade and become just another torn page in a dusty history book."*

**— Michael M. Cochran**

# Pure and Simple

Growing up Gullah in Awendaw in the 1950s was a great life. My father had a small farm and garden where we lived off the land, grew our own vegetables, and raised chickens and hogs. This life was so pure and simple!

Even though we didn't know it, we were growing and eating some of the healthiest foods, like okra, tomatoes, cucumbers, and butter beans. At night, we unshelled beans as the elders told stories. We bought almost everything at the Charleston market, and the fishermen would stroll through the neighborhood selling their catch of the day. There is nothing fresher than this seafood nowadays!

My mother was a great cook and influenced me greatly in my desire to become a chef. As I closed one chapter as an office manager, I began cooking professionally and later opened the Gullah Cuisine Restaurant. After twenty years of restaurant ownership, I co-authored my cookbook and memoir, *Gullah Cuisine: By Land and By Sea*. I closed Gullah Cuisine in 2014, and now I spend my days in my hometown of Awendaw, waking up smelling fresh wild flowers, looking at the trees, and listening to the harmony of the birds, bull frogs and crickets.

---

**Charlotte Jenkins**
Owner and Chef, Gullah Cuisine
Author, *Gullah Cuisine: By Land and By Sea*

*Bridge to Harmony. Photo by Michelle Bolton*

*Morris Island Lighthouse. Photo by Charles Merry*

# Telling a Good Story

As a politician's daughter, a professional writer, promoter, and event planner, I often find myself selling the city. Don't get me wrong; it's not a hard job. Well, at least not to anyone who has been here to visit. This is because as soon as visitors hit the downtown streets or the Cooper River Bridge, they instantly see the beauty.

To me, Charleston is so many things. First it is history, but really *my* history. I could drive around anywhere and share a story, talk about an outing, or what I was doing at a set year and time at a particular location. There are the spots like Charles Towne Landing, the original birthplace of the state. As a child, it was a place we frequented for events and races. In honesty, Charles Towne Landing was taken for granted until Hurricane Hugo nearly destroyed it. For a long time after the storm, the park was near abandoned. When a group of politicians took notice and secured proper funding, it gained the attention it deserved. Now the pathways overlook the beauty of the downtown skyline as it winds along the Ashley River. Indigenous animals fill the zoo, and the tall ship replica has properly been restored. If there is one place I recommend visiting, it is this historic gem.

And then, of course, there's the water. I was raised at the beach, and was spoiled by my grandparent's house on the creek. Grandpa was a fisherman, and he taught us how to bait a pole and string a crab trap. The reward was always big: local, fresh seafood, the kind grandma would instantly freeze or fry in a pan with Crisco. Even though they have both since passed away, we still get to spend our days at the same spot they left behind for our family. Its salty air and foamy surf is cleansing to the soul, and it is the one place I find solace in the city.

Another perk of life in Charleston is its food. Eating and drinking well is a given here. Over the last ten years, budding talented chefs have descended from all over and opened up some of the country's best restaurants and bars. It's not all high-end either. Some of the best places to eat are local dives like Bowen's Island, where steamed oysters are shoveled onto newspaper covered tables under a screened porch overlooking the creek. Equally delightful are the soul food sensations like Bertha's, where sisters line up daily and serve family recipes they learned as children—okra stew, fried chicken, macaroni and cheese, and cornbread. And Charleston boasts many venues that serve the local farmers' and fishermen's finest bounty.

The people here are pretty special, too. Not to sound snobbish, but if someone is born and raised in Charleston, they have a special pride and connection to the city. We are also typically good storytellers (do not call us gossipers, please). We are welcoming and will give you something to eat and drink the minute you walk into our homes. We love having fun and struggle with working a full 40-hour week. Sign us up for any chance to party and socialize. We love to remember the good ole days and often reminisce about the times that have come and gone. But we also love the new generation moving in and appreciate the diversity, culture, and experiences they bring to this great city.

There are many things to love about Charleston, but its history, water, food, and people make this city so special to me, and make me proud to call this place home.

---

**Angel Passailaigue Postell**
Owner, Home Team Public Relations and Events
and Charleston City Editor, *The Daily Meal*

Photo by Andrew Cebulka

*Charleston Abstract. Photo by Karen M. Peluso*

*South Battery Street in Summer. Photo by Charles Merry*

# The Land of My Heart

Dear Lowcountry,

I came to you determined not to love you, those many years ago. I accompanied my parents on a visit to Charleston, where my father was a candidate for a prestigious position at the Medical University. They were wined, and they were dined; I was thrown collectively to the wolves known as the children of the faculty entertaining my parents. At least, that's how I saw it. I was the girl from off (and from a northern "off" at that), injected into the adolescent South of Broad social scene at the insistence of parents. Sitting on the side piazza, the balmy night air was a far cry from the air back home, frigid with the coming of winter. I don't know whether it was the cadence of the talk around me, or the scents of unfamiliar blossoms and sea-tinged air that recalled joyful vacation days, but my heart softened. As the gathering shifted to another home, I got a guided tour of a small corner of the city. The cobbled stones of Church Street and the little beach revealed by the Ashley River at low tide enchanted me, though I confess, I don't recall the name of the boy who walked with me. When we flew back to winter and my old life, the scents and sights of Charleston clung to me, and have never let go.

It was here I learned to lure a crab from the creek behind our home into the cooking pot, to cast a shrimp net, and marvel at the moods of the wetlands that embrace the coast. Here, I learned that a palmetto is a thing of pride, and definitely not a palm tree; I learned how to tell a white heron from a snowy egret, and what a joggling board is. I became a girl of the beaches: Folly, Sullivan's Island, Isle of Palms: each had a separate joy and beauty. I memorized which house along Murray Blvd. you pointed the bow of a boat toward if you were crossing the Ashley River from James Island to the peninsula. I learned that pluff mud can get on your clothes, between your toes, and its distinct smell in your nose, but also in your soul. I lingered in Shell House at Ashley Hall, with my friends, girls who became women I still delight in being with and cherish as friends.

I left you, Lowcountry, for my studies at several universities and to travel the world, but when I decided to find a spot to call home as a young adult, out on my own, it was Charleston that again called me. I was welcomed back; the fathers of friends I knew in high school were now the physicians I worked with as I embarked on my nursing career. Their generosity giving supplies, medicines, and money to a small medical clinic in rural India where I spent a summer as a volunteer still warms my heart. And when I came back from that trip, and met the man of my dreams, I remember how several of these same physicians insisted on vetting him, since my own daddy had passed on.

Charleston was the city of our courtship and though I left you again to gather a graduate degree, we came back here to raise our family. Charleston

embraced the return of an adopted daughter and the man from "off" that she loved. We introduced our son to the beauties of Lowcountry living. His eyes would light up in wonder at the glory of the ACE basin from canoe, or the mysteries of Four Hole Swamp. Together, we would watch from the porch as thunderheads rolled across the sky. "Better even than television," he once declared, and he was right. Our home in the historic district was our haven, a multi-generational family, for my mother came to live with us, and my siblings would tumble in for extended visits.

It was here that I found my stride as a pediatric clinical nurse specialist. When I developed an illness that nearly killed me, and forced me to give up my practice, it was in the arms of the Lowcountry, amidst the live oaks and wildlife, that I was able to find a balance. Now in a stable health state, and able to be more active, I've tried to give back in the ways I can. My love of books and reading has lead me to volunteerism at school libraries, at Charleston Country Public Library, Charleston Library Society, Trident Literacy Association, and to spreading free books via BookCrossing. I like to "live local," supporting the craftsmen and women of the Lowcountry. I've learned the names of the farmers whose bounty fills our bellies, the artists and artisans whose works grace our home, the coffee roasters and chefs whose establishments are the spots to which I take visitors for refreshment. I have my favorite places to show off on a tour of the city, some of which, like the Unitarian Church graveyard, I recently learned that our son, living now on the other coast, recommends to people he knows who visit Charleston. (Second generation pride makes me smile). Here my heart dances and my soul sings, each to many different tunes and melodies, as different as a sassy salsa to a Mozart motet. As I move into another phase of life, as an artist, I even know the names of the hens whose eggs I use to create Pysanky (Ukrainian style eggs).

Ah, Lowcountry, thank you. Our romance has lasted nearly 45 years, and will go on until my last breath. You may not be the land of my birth, but you are the land of my heart.

---

**Amy Romanczuk**
Pysanky and psanky-inspired design artist
Courtesy of bookczuk.blogspot.com and lowcountryloveletters.com, an online publication by Angela Wicke and Emily Gildea

Photo by Alan Romanczuk

*Evening on the Wando.* Photo by Michelle Bolton

# Island Time

If we allow, life in the Lowcountry moves in a small circle. After many moons on the North Carolina coast I've now called Charleston home for nine years, letting its familiarity spin around every season. I seek out and find small coastal villages in the same schedule—from Awendaw to Edisto, Meggett to McClellanville, Six-mile to SeeWee. For me, these salt-worn, cyclical places define coastal South Carolina.

With May busting green and warm out of the trees, we don't need long sleeves and jeans between fishing holes. We don't need our white boots and bibs. Raccoon eyes glow in sunburned faces. The scales over at Haddrell's are hanging again, slimier than before.

We focus on wind direction as much as work, tide as closely as time; moon phase is as important as e-mail. We knock off at five and go to the river in johnboats, spinning the dried-out cast net, getting it salty again. With a few baits and a few grubs, the green-tipped grass calls us to an old creek, and a handful of spring trout pull hard on light rods.

Just the same, winter kingfishing under gunmetal skies has turned hot and feverish, with mackerel showing at ten miles and their Spanish cousins making a first appearance. Drone spoons are replaced by the big pogies on the beach, hounded by pelicans, dogged again by center-consoles and 12-foot cast-nets. Cobia patrol tidelines. Blackfin tuna chew beyond the break.

Fishing tournament schedules grind into work and weddings, their names ringing with the memory of some big leaping blue fish, or some long night in a marina party tent. Hatteras, Big Rock, Wrightsville, Pirates Cove. Edisto, Bohicket, Megadock, Georgetown. If you could, you'd fish them all.

And so, every day builds toward the next. Bigger fish loom with each rising degree of water temperature. New birds arrive with every storm front. More medicine blows in on every afternoon sea breeze. And we hustle through the oak-lined streets, trailering up, waving to everyone, and icing down the coolers for an evening jaunt.

Through the cold winter, life was a ragged edge of chilly wind and hard work. Everything was dull and brown. Most of the critters were dormant. Now the air thumps with summer heat. Life is a rolled-down window, a little cash from the ATM, a cold beer after a long sunburn. Life is a big grackle squawking in the longleaf pine, an osprey whistling to her young, an owl answering a crow.

Life is a lively bait well, an organized tackle box, a well-tuned motor. It's busting fish under showered glass minnows, night wind whistling through a screen, the first mosquito slapped on a red arm.

Life is a breakfast restaurant that knows what you want, a pelican that meets you at the dock, a school of fish that shows up on time, a tideline that marks the bite. It's a handful of close friends that share the best spots, or a fishing partner who'd disown you if you mentioned that other place.

The world moves cyber-fast these days, sweeping by and changing so quickly we've almost forgotten what it's like to slow down. It may be that the freeway rush catches every haunt from Folly to Dewees. Some people say as Florida goes and the beaches off New Jersey and Cape Cod change, so go the Carolinas. But I'd like to think otherwise. Tomorrow's Saturday, and I'll be somewhere between breakfast and a flounder, worrying about as little as possible.

---

**Douglas Cutting**
Vice President of Garden & Gun Land,
outdoor writer and sportsman

Shem Creek Shrimpers. Photo by Amelia Weaver

# Yearning and Learning

I moved to Charleston with purpose, to leave behind the hustle and bustle of the manic North and establish a career as a chef with a deliberate slower pace. Twenty years ago, a fraternity of chefs owned this town, but not in a pretentious "world's best" kind of way ... in a respectful "I paid my dues" sort of way. A hierarchy of talent existed, and those who had the most popular restaurants were those who climbed the culinary ranks on their own. We didn't have publicists. We had reputations, and Charleston kept our secret for

*Angel Oak Tree.* Photo by Steven Hyatt

as long as she possibly could. We threw cast nets, and we wet our own lines. We picked, and we harvested. We served, and we cleaned. We prepped lines, and we expedited. We tended bar, and we knew every customer. We learned from the best, and the best learned from us. We didn't yearn to be exclusive. We yearned to be recommended by our peers, appreciated by our staff, and most of all, recognized with kind words from our patrons. That camaraderie among chefs remains, and our biggest fans are each other. I just hope it lasts. Man, I hope it lasts.

**Brett McKee**
CEO of McKee's at 139B

Photo by Michelle Bolton

# Family, Friends and Fans

One of my earliest memories of Charleston is listening to my dad play his guitar for family and friends on Sullivan's Island in the early 1970s. Though it was nearly 50 years ago, I remember frolicking on the beach that day, trick-or-treating that Halloween night, and watching the iconic lighthouse, known as the Charleston Light, shine its protective beam on the unpredictable Atlantic and The Holy City's majestic harbor.

For years we rented a beach house that was literally steps away from that lighthouse, and I was consistently mesmerized by the glow that illuminated the starry sky. My dad, Poppa Futch, would sing songs and tell stories with his friend Mag Greenthaler, who would accompany him on the gut bucket, a galvanized bucket that Charleston shrimpers, oyster men, and fishermen still use today. This bucket was turned upside down, with a string tied to the tip of a plow handle or broomstick and an eyebolt drilled through its center. It was an instrument similar to the bass fiddle that would resonate when the rope was plucked. Together they entertained family, friends, and customers, sharing a sentiment that many good-natured Charlestonians believe: "There are no strangers here, only family and friends who haven't yet met."

Charlestonians loved Poppa Futch's music then and continue to love his music today when he plays with me, my brother, Hal and my band, Blue Dogs. Many often request that he play a song he didn't write but made his own, "Homegrown Tomatoes." Once, he received a standing ovation when he walked onstage, before even playing the first chord or singing the first note. Okay, so I'm a little proud of my dad. But I think this story speaks volumes about the respect and good nature that Charlestonians have shown me, my family, and all of my bands, Futch Brothers, Blue Dogs and Occasional Milkshake.

I've been entertaining folks in Charleston for many years, playing in the many bars, restaurants, dives, music venues, events, weddings, and, yes, even a few funerals. I love playing music, but feel especially vested in Charleston. Blue Dogs, a band of 27 years and counting, hosts an annual anniversary show at The Charleston Music Hall, which has become a reunion of our music compadres, family, friends, and fans. I'm reminded during these December shows of just how blessed I have been, first of all, to have a dad who instilled his love of music and entertaining in me, and, second, to have the pleasure of playing music for all those loyal and devoted fans.

Our fans have supported my Blue Dogs partner, Bobby Houck and me all these years, whether it be at Back Market Café, The Windjammer, a sandy floor in a horse barn, or the parlor of one of downtown Charleston's finest homes.

Since my days at the College of Charleston, my life has played out in this wonderful city as a musician and entertainer, and over the last ten years, as a realtor. I love the smell of the marsh and the beaches, even when you can't see them. I love Lowcountry Boil, a meal likely harvested within just a few miles from wherever you are in Charleston. I love the camaraderie of an oyster roast and hearing John G. Thornhill's voice command attention from the table when he shouts, "Hot Oysters!"

On Sullivan's Island that Halloween night years ago, the stage was the backyard. The ocean echoed a cadence that would beat in my heart for a lifetime. Each time I'm afforded the chance to see that split second flash of light that radiates over the harbor, I'm reminded that each passing day is a blessing. Charleston will forever be my home, and my audience will always be friends and family.

**Hank Futch**
Bassist and founding member, Blue Dogs

Photo by Austin Nelson

*Really Living. Photo by Terry Knight*

"Like each grounded piling set firmly beneath the sand, the people of Charleston represent enduring strength in waves of storms and tragedy. As we walk united atop her pier, may we always be grateful for her foundation."

*Folly Beach. Photo by Janet Garrity*

# Home at the 'Joe'

Twenty seasons ago, the River-Dogs began a wonderful run in the Joseph P. Riley, Jr. Park, one of the sweetest diamonds in all of Minor League Baseball. At the topping off ceremony, Mayor Riley spoke, not about the state of the art HOK-designed gem on the banks of the Ashley River, but about baseball. He spoke of grandchildren learning about the game from people eager to pass their passion for life and for the game to those whom they loved the most.

*Bill Murray and Joe Riley playing around.*

"I watched games here with my mom and dad. Your brother learned to play the game at College Park. That was his ... this is yours," Riley said.

Without being preachy or pedantic, he set a code of conduct for us to follow, more specifically for the leadership team of the Dogs to follow. It was our job to create memories for the citizens of greater Charleston. Our job was to have fun and create laughter. The natural by-product would be warmth.

You, citizens of Charleston, are the caretakers of our games and our joy.

"A community center where the real product is human interaction," Riley said.

I hope we have lived up to his charge. We have tried; with 1500 South Atlantic League games, 800 Citadel games, hundreds of concerts and countless community

events later, his words still reverberate in my ears, probably my soul.

"Michael, we have a responsibility to the people for whom this wonderful building was built," Riley said.

Over the years, we have been the merchants of laughter, the peddlers of silly and the stewards of the national pastime.

As Mayor Riley and I both gaze into one of the exploding pinwheels of light that only a Friday night baseball game on the Ashley can provide, I hope history will say that we built a yard of the people, by the people, but mostly for the people. I hope that we have left the city and indeed the region, better than we found them. I know it has profoundly impacted the Veeck family. We came as strangers.

**Mike Veeck**
President, Charleston RiverDogs

Photos courtesy of the Charleston RiverDogs.

*Mist Morning. Photo by Kelley Luikey*

*The Harbor's Welcome. Photo by Charles Merry*

# To It All, and More

Growing up on the peninsula of Charleston means so much to me that it is hard to describe in words. I've watched Charleston morph into the city that it is today, and this causes me to stop and remember myself as a child, engulfed in the beauty of our historic neighborhoods. I remember my mother taking me way uptown to Robinson's Bike Shop (where the Basil restaurant is now on upper King Street) to get my first Earth Cruiser with a basket on the front so I could deliver *The Evening Post*. I would fold papers on the steps of the East Bay Playground after football practice, and I always looked forward to every other Friday afternoon when the bartender lady at Henry's on North Market Street would pay me $5 for her subscription. I would immediately use the money to go buy some gourmet popcorn on South Market Street. Navigating the narrow alleys of oddly-shaped and surfaced streets in the city on my big bicycle created an infrastructural maze that made delivering newspapers to oddly-shaped piazzas and throwing papers into hidden gardens so much fun. It was daily target practice. When I think about my first job and learning the value of a dollar, I think about Charleston.

Memories of our bicycle gangs around town remind me of making stops at the corner grocery stores, which were our hangouts. These stores are not as commonplace anymore, but they added so much to my childhood. Mr. Lehrman's on Bull and Smith Streets and Mr. Burbage's Corner Grocery and Lakeside Drug Store on Broad Street, those were our hangouts. Mr. Burbage used to put me in timeout next to the meat counter when I was acting up. He saw me get my first driver's license and saw me go off to college and then to law school. When I think about our old neighborhood in Charleston, I fondly remember these local hangouts.

The soundtrack of Charleston in my youth is any Sting or Police song with some U2, REM, Neil Young, Crosby Stills & Nash, and Michael Jackson sprinkled in. Being from Charleston meant being exposed to the arts at an early age, from music during Spoleto, to acting classes and performances at the Dock Street Theatre, to band practice in a local warehouse for hours on end, to getting that first gig at Cumberlands, Myskins, or the old Music Farm. When I was a teenager, I did a radio interview at 96 Wave with The Wood Man Bartlett, and the experience ignited a passion for playing live music. When I think of my appreciation for art, music, and storytelling, I think of Charleston.

As my Fat & Juicy Cocktail Mixer business partner, John Glen and I recently surmised, a toast to Charleston generally means this: To being extraordinary. To that time of year. To the first tailgate of football season. To oyster roasts. To pig pickin's. To flip flops and no socks. To long docks. To salty water. To hanging out on the boat until dusk. To shrimping and crabbing all day. To black tie affairs. To bow ties. To sun dresses. To porch parties. To garden parties. To seersucker. To oyster-colored poplin suits. To Barbour jackets. To not being late to church. To sunny, humid days. To Sunday brunch with our families. To Holy City bells ringing every 15 minutes. To water skiing all day. To high tide and rain and flooded streets. To the sweet flower ladies. To being sun-kissed. To the sound of horseshoes hittin' the pavement. To the smell of paper mills and road apples. To turning the radio up and ripping the knob off. To not being afraid of having fun. To life and to love. To Charleston!

---

**Joe Good, III**
Managing partner, Good Law Group and
Vice President, Fat & Juicy Cocktail Mixers

*A Pathway to Home. Photo by Martha Lawrence*

*A Working Man's Creek. Photo by Charles Merry*

# Southern Paradox

I first moved to Charleston in March of 1996. I grew up in Charlotte and was trying to get a job with a newspaper somewhere in North or South Carolina. Before moving to Charleston, I was visiting Colorado, ostensibly interviewing with *The Daily Camera*, but actually following Widespread Panic. The temperature in Boulder the night I left was minus 6. The temperature in Charleston when I arrived was plus 60.

I started as an obit clerk at *The Post and Courier*, working from 3 to 11 pm. After my shift I would go out. South Carolina still had the mini-bottle blue law, and waitresses would get off work and order "Four Purple Hooters six ways"—8 mini-bottles mixed and poured out for six shots.

Though it had become passé elsewhere, kids here still walked the sidewalk blasting music from boomboxes. To pick someone up at the sleepy airport with its seventies brown brick, you'd leave the car at the curb and meet them at the gate. There was a Woolworth's on King that sold paper towels and underwear and goldfish.

The Citadel Library, since renovated, looked like the set of a Wes Anderson film. The top of the round Holiday Inn, now a bland hotel restaurant, was an 80s disco bar.

I write this not as an elegy to the past, nor to complain that Charleston has become, as I heard a kid say recently "too bougie" (with a soft g, as in bourgeois), but more to show how long it held out, and still does. The Confederate Home on Broad Street is an ancient oasis. Morris Sokol furniture just closed, but there's Dixie across the street, and there's Wulbern-Koval, where you can still get typewriter ribbon, and Read Brothers, which sells fabric and hi-fi systems.

I like to think Charleston will always be a strange old town, because it's a Southern city, and a Southern city is by nature a paradox. Southerners are supposed to be pastoral; they eschew tight spaces and don't parallel park to run into the corner store. So Charleston, with so much Southernness crammed into three square miles, should, in theory, be too Southern to be Southern.

Instead it's become a beacon, a showroom of Southern style. Charlestonians have always been very proud of their city, and sooner or later outsiders were going to start to take notice. When you preserve an amazing collection of buildings, sit on a harbor next to five beaches, and throw in Spoleto, Wine + Food Fest, Shepard Fairey, Stephen Colbert and Bill Murray, it's just a matter of time before you have people paying $600 for a hotel room.

It may seem ideal to live where others vacation, but most Charlestonians don't hit the spa every day and dine on veal sweetbreads every night. As Scott and Zelda Fitzgerald's daughter Scottie once said about her parents: "Fascinating, brilliant and often charming, but they should be sat next to at dinner parties, not lived with."

For me the rare beauty of Charleston is found not in the grand houses on Legare or the private gardens, but in those trying to make an ordinary life in an extraordinary place. If you look for them, you'll see little haiku glimpses of a unique humanity, the exposed beams of the structure of a real, working city.

The cook having a beer at The Griffon, a sheath of knives under his arm. The carriage driver reading Tom Robbins in her Confederate uniform. The meter maid taking abuse from a red-faced SUV. Valet parkers in full sprint. And the Rue de Jean waitress, in the gravel parking lot by the dumpster, eating *coq au vin* out of a Styrofoam tray. After work she'll take off her black apron and go out on Upper King with her friends. Although it's more likely bespoke cocktails or single-barrel bourbons now, and although the mini-bottle blue law is gone, I still like to think she'll order four shots six ways.

---

**By Jonathan Sanchez**
Owner of Blue Bicycle Books and Director of YALLFest

Photo by Lauren Sanchez

*King Street from on high. Photo by Tim Sayer*

Street Arts. Photo by Janet Garrity

# Engaging in Life and Art

I grew up in the historic rice growing region of the Lowcountry of South Carolina. While my career as a professional artist based in Chicago, Illinois and Naples, Florida, took me throughout Europe and the Far East, I always returned to my roots near Gardens Corner, South Carolina several times a year. During my trips home, I always visited my favorite city in the world, Charleston, South Carolina. It is this city's heritage, which has evolved throughout the last 250 years, that feeds my creative energies, ignites my imagination, and fosters my social interests, civic commitments, respect for humanity, and love for a culture that embraces African, European, and Native American visual, performing, and culinary arts.

Six years ago I had the opportunity and privilege of moving to Charleston to make it my permanent home and studio. My studio provides me a place where I can paint, in an atmosphere that affords me the space, privacy, and dignity to challenge my creative energies. At the same time, I can leave the studio and not have to drive, but just walk throughout the streets and experience the culinary delights of specialty restaurants serving incredibly prepared foods from almost every cultural and ethnic makeup imaginable. I can continue walking and meet with visitors, friends, and associates at numerous boutique and internationally known hotels. These meetings encourage meaningful dialogues about issues, ideas, and concepts that help us keep a focus on life, culture, challenges, and events.

I thrive on the array of museums and historical preservations sites in Charleston, such as the Gibbes Museum of Art and exhibitions at the Waterfront City Gallery run by the Charleston Department of Cultural Affairs. Another highlight of Charleston life that engages my spirit are the performances held at the Gaillard Auditorium, Dock Street Theatre, TD Arena, Marion Square, Hampton Park, and many other venues and festivals that showcase choirs, such as the Colour of Music, Spoleto, Moja Arts Festival, Wine & Food Festival, Piccolo Spoleto and others.

Charleston is one of those rare cities that strives to reach out and engage residents and visitors from all social, economic, ethnic, racial and cultural groups that want to contribute to culture and society. This is why I love this city.

**Jonathan Green**
Painter of the Southern Experience and
Creator of Cross-Cultural Fine Art

Photo by Charlie Allen Smith

*Established in 1748 by nineteen young gentlemen of various trades and professions wishing to avail themselves of the latest publications from Great Britain, the Charleston Library Society paved the way for the founding of the College of Charleston in 1770 and provided the core collection of natural history artifacts for the founding of the Charleston Museum (the first in America) in 1773. In 1914 the Library Society moved to its current location at 164 King Street. This was the first building to house the collection that was designed and built for the Society. Here, in the new building, members like DuBose Heyward, John Bennett, Beatrice Witte Ravenel, Albert Simons, Josephine Pinckney, and many others, studied and read and wrote, diligently weaving the cultural fabric of twentieth century Charleston. Photo by Martha Lawrence*

# Running the Race

I had a full childhood which began in Wagener Terrace, a neighborhood in Charleston, South Carolina, where I was raised with my three siblings. We lived very close to our school, and Hampton Park was our playground. My grandparents and some of my cousins lived right across the street, and my grandfather introduced me to playing fun pranks on the rest of the family. This became a family tradition. My grandfather's house on the Isle of Palms was the gathering place for all of our relatives, and from there we would take boat rides to Goat Island when nobody lived there but the "goat man and goat lady." I made some close friendships back then that have lasted throughout my life. We played touch-football, half-rubber and basketball, which gave me that taste for sports and physical activity.

My parent's passion for horticulture was contagious and instilled in me the simple joy of watching things grow and the great feeling of accomplishment that comes with it. When I was around 13 years old, they built me a greenhouse to help cultivate my interest in plants; it became a life-long passion. When I attended Charleston Southern University to study business, I earned extra money by selling plants out of my greenhouse, and eventually found some property on Johns Island to plant eucalyptus trees; this endeavor became part of my entrepreneurial plan. After various jobs, I was hired in the Student Aid office of the Medical University of South Carolina, the beginning of an ongoing relationship. The job lasted for about 15 years. I then became Director of The Wellness Center at MUSC in 1988, which exposed me to the athletic world as a business. This led to my becoming the Director of Corporate Development for the MUSC Children's Hospital, a cause that will always remain near and dear to my heart. Then came an experience that further deepened my connection to Charleston: Hurricane Hugo. The hurricane hit the coast, and the damage to life and property, including my own farm, was devastating. As a child, my friends and I thought hurricanes were exciting and fun, but after Hugo, I finally understood the power of nature and man's inability to control it. It was a rude awakening. I saw our city come together during this tragedy, and I was overcome with pride for our community.

While working at the Wellness Center, I was asked to help with a modestly successful event, the Cooper River Bridge Run. It was like coming home! I felt this was the ultimate challenge for my honed skills, and the idea of growing the race in my hometown, while raising money for charities, appealed to me greatly. There aren't many places that can compete with the beauty of Charleston Harbor and the boundless energy of the Charleston people; we tapped into that energy. We began getting corporate sponsors and adding events to the Bridge Run weekend. It is now on its 39th year, and has grown from 6,000 to an average of 40,000 participants. We're proud that our grant program sponsors hundreds of school-aged children so that they can participate in the festivities. The Bridge Run is the third largest 10k in the country and brings in millions of dollars in revenue to Charleston and the surrounding areas. The involvement of approximately 4,000 volunteers, the staff, and the community spirit is what makes this event so successful; that's what Charleston is all about.

I would say that life in Charleston has taught me to work hard, play hard, and stay positive. Never look back, and forgive but don't forget!

**Julian Smith**
Executive Race Director, Cooper River Bridge Run

Photo by Jenn Cady

*Bridge, Another Angle. Photo by Robbie Silver*

*Catching it. Photo by Tim Sayer*

# Black Cloth

Racism,
let us no longer walk in your shoes.
You are a traveler of darkness, a walker of shadows,
cloaking yourself in a black cloth like the grim reaper
and arming your soul with the tools of a terrorist—
a misguided soldier who's trying to start a war.

My sisters,
heaven was as close as your breath that night.
You came to Mother Emanuel to worship in the glow of God,
and speak the light that flows from love.
How beautiful of Him to hear your words
and lift you into the arms of Christ.

My brothers,
you walked toward heaven with focus,
even when your shoes were stained with the dirt of intolerance.
A black cloth lays silent at Clementa's seat, resting under
a single rose. It was taken from our city's soil,
where seeds of faith continue to grow.

Charleston,
I see heaven in your tears and feel the weight of sadness
in your voice. I've seen strangers hold hands
as the sun wraps us in unbearable heat,
I've watched children of contradiction come together
for the unity of the Holy City.

South Carolina,
nine members of your family are now in heaven
and you have to confront the reality of racism,
the dusk of pain, the lightlessness of the dawn.
Because I would rather hang a black cloth
on a flag pole
than give the Confederate flag
another glimpse of the sun.

– MA

**Marcus Amaker**
Poet, Graphic Designer,
Videographer and Musician

Photo by Lisa Livingston

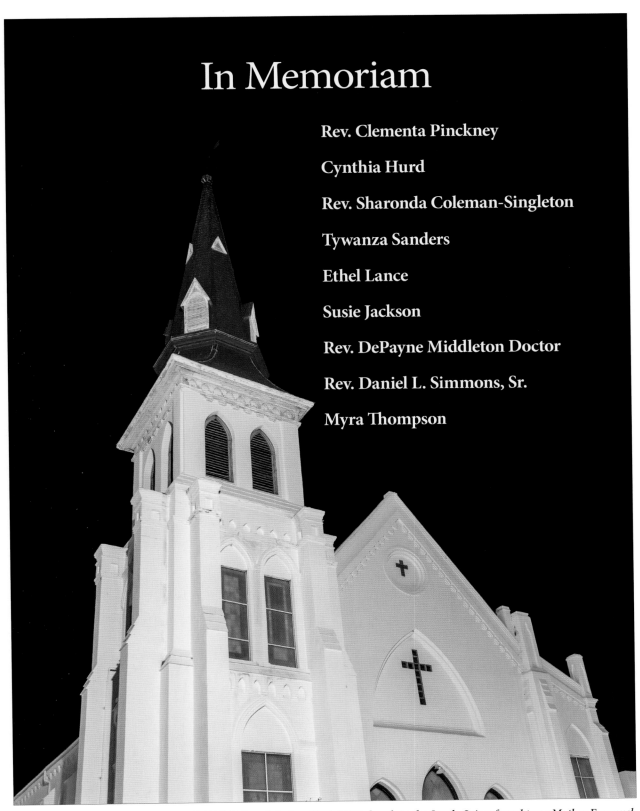

# In Memoriam

Rev. Clementa Pinckney

Cynthia Hurd

Rev. Sharonda Coleman-Singleton

Tywanza Sanders

Ethel Lance

Susie Jackson

Rev. DePayne Middleton Doctor

Rev. Daniel L. Simmons, Sr.

Myra Thompson

*Emanuel African Methodist Episcopal (AME) Church is the oldest AME church in the South. It is referred to as Mother Emanuel. Emanuel has one of the largest and oldest black congregations south of Baltimore, Maryland. The AME Church has never strayed from the course charted by Richard Allen. The church is wedded to the spiritual doctrine of "God our Father, Christ our Redeemer, Man our Brother." Photo by Delk Haigler*

*Botany Bay Hero. Photo by Tripp Smith*

*Sol Legre Flats. Photo by Tripp Smith*

"To some degree, life here has always revolved around the water. From boneyards and beaches, from creeks and salt marsh, from the rivers to the ocean, the water is a large part of Charleston's soul."

*Thunder Head. Photo by Tripp Smith*

*Beach Life. Photo by Tim Sayer*

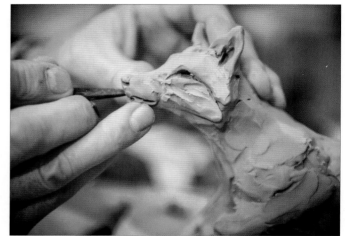

# Wild at Art

I am often asked what makes SEWE so successful. The first attribute is the easiest—we host our event in the city of Charleston. Second, we invite some of the best artists and exhibitors in the country and the world to the city of Charleston. That's one recipe for success. Our staff, the backbone of SEWE, is proprietary about the show and its outcome. We all call Charleston home, so it's important to us to offer the most sincere hospitality and deliver a world class event. Since I began my tenure in 1987, SEWE has grown exponentially. Thanks to our young staff, we continue to change with the times and technologies and strive to keep things fresh. Our success is due to the overwhelming support we receive from local and visiting attendees, artists, exhibitors and especially our corporate supporters. But the true testament to the Exposition's glory is her host, the most beautiful and embracing city in the world … Charleston.

**Jimmy Huggins**
President, Southeastern Wildlife
Exposition (SEWE)

*Flight! The Center for Birds of Prey in Awendaw operates a professional avian medical clinic for injured birds of prey and some shorebird species. The center offers on-site and outreach educational programs to students and adults. It also conducts relevant field and laboratory research studies. Photo by Elizabeth Sher*

*Spoleto Festival USA Opening Ceremonies. Photo by Julia Lynn*

# An Italian Vision, Our Cultural Arts

When Gian Carlo Menotti first visited Charleston in 1976, he found a city with everything that visitors expect of Charleston—beautiful, if somewhat shabby mansions, cobblestone streets and mountains of history —but he was looking for something else. He had come to find a city where a counterpart to the Festival of Two Worlds, a festival he founded in Spoleto, Italy in 1958, could take place.

At first, the search had taken members of the festival staff to various cities up the Hudson River near New York City, close enough to be convenient for New York based audiences and artists. However, in discussions with Walter Anderson, director of the music program at the National Endowment for the Arts, they were persuaded to look for a place more like Spoleto, Italy, a town that had been economically and culturally rich at one time, but had fallen on hard times starting in the mid-nineteenth century. Anderson encouraged them to look at cities in the South where a Spoleto Festival could bring its unique combination of opera, dance, music, theater and visual arts to a part of the country where these performances and exhibitions would be a revelation. A festival in the South could also serve as an economic engine, much as the Festival of Two Worlds had done in Spoleto, Italy.

Among the first stops that Menotti made on that visit to Charleston was the Dock Street Theatre. Built in 1935 on the site of the first theater built in the American colonies, the Dock Street Theatre, even with its name, conjured up an earlier time in Charleston when the first opera performed in the colonies took place on that first stage. With its cypress paneling, its intimacy and its great acoustics, Menotti, a two-time Pulitzer Prize winner for his operas, decided that this theater would be perfect for the chamber music and small operas that were an essential part of the festival program. He then visited the Gaillard Auditorium which would become the site for the grand operas, the large ballet companies and the orchestral concerts that enriched the festival program. The Cistern Yard at the College of Charleston with its Spanish moss-covered live oaks would be a perfect venue for outdoor concerts and the beautiful gardens at Middleton Place would be the perfect setting for a final concert to end the festival each year. The city's many churches, parks and grand public buildings would also serve as a backdrop to a festival that needed a beautiful setting in which to thrive.

Menotti knew that Charleston was the setting for *Porgy and Bess*, the quintessential American opera but on that first visit he didn't know how rich Charleston's cultural history had been. In addition to the first purpose-built theater, Charleston could boast a ballet company in the eighteenth century, the oldest musical organization in the country, and a series of house concerts in the early nineteenth century that were reported on by newspapers as far away as New York.

Over the years, the festival he established in 1977, Spoleto Festival USA, has followed the example of the Italian festival by including grand opera, chamber music and theater. It has added those special legacies of Charleston—it has explored both jazz and the music of the sea islands. That first opera, *Flora*, has been revived for the Dock Street Theatre; the music of Johann Pachelbel whose son was the organist at St. Philip's Church has enlivened the chamber music program; an operetta composed by the son of the founder of the Jenkins Orphanage will receive its world premiere at the festival.

In Charleston, Spoleto Festival USA not only found a home, it found an inspiration.

---

**Nigel Redden**
General Director of Spoleto Festival USA

Photo by Peter Frank Edwards

# Rights by Association

Where are you from? It's conversational currency item #2, preceded only by your name. Both have presented problems for me since birth. After stating—and then re-pronouncing—my first name, I'm then forced to drop the 'Navy family' excuse. Forever, I am a boy with no hometown.

But since 2003, whenever I'm not at home, I state with pride that I am from Charleston. More specifically, I'm from Folly Beach.

Here though—in the place I consider home—I'll always be from an ambiguous 'off.' In Maine, you can spend one winter and claim it forever, but here in Charleston, you've got one chance—birth—to get it right.

So I claim rights by association. My wife was born here. She grew up on the Isle of Palms and graduated from Ashley Hall, and after leaving for college, assumed she'd never move back. She tried New York and Boulder and was headed for Miami until I reeled her in. She fought hard—and I was willing to jump in and swim with her—but in the end, we landed on Folly, the first place in my life that ever scratched my travel bug bite enough to satiate the itch.

I first discovered Charleston in seventh grade, when dad was the rector of an Episcopal church in Darlington, South Carolina (post-Navy). Even today, when I drive through the mossy tunnel of live oaks on Bohicket Road to go visit my folks on Seabrook Island, I get the same reflexive butterflies I experienced en route to Camp Saint Christopher as a nervous 12-year-old about to be thrown into a seaside world of wonder, populated by friendly strangers.

While at Davidson College, a freshman year girlfriend reintroduced me to the city. The first time I visited her family, we drove across I-526 toward Mount Pleasant, and the vast vistas of marsh and creek settled into my mind like deep magic. For the next three years, I made a habit of convincing friends on Friday nights that hopping in the car and heading to the coast was a fine idea. We'd wake up the next morning in the dunes at the east end of Folly, already sunburned, and toast to the splendor of the Morris Island Lighthouse with whatever restoratives we'd packed.

It was back to Camp Saint Christopher after college for a year of teaching coastal ecology. My work days were spent neck deep in the 'mud pit,' catching crabs with rope and chicken necks off the dock, and traipsing through the maritime forest with a keen eye peeled for water mocs. On weekends, I'd paddle to remote islands and converse with sea otters, egrets and black tip sharks, getting lost deep in the maze of low tide marshes in the ACE Basin.

I wandered to California and fell in love with the Sierra Nevada, returned home for another wrong girl, scooted back off to Maine, and came home again, this time to write for the *Charleston City Paper*.

A year into my first real job, I was yearning for adventure. My lease ended in West Ashley, and I thought about splitting for the West Coast, when I met two sisters who needed a roommate in their beachfront rental shack—one of the last—on Folly Beach.

I moved in and promptly got kicked out by the wine-loving would-be-pirate landlord (fittingly known as Captain Jack), but I didn't go far.

Seven houses and nine years later, I'm still here, even pulling off a post-wedding coup that landed an Isle of Palms native on Folly. And house number seven—a cottage built in 1940 with just enough room for a small family—is ours to keep.

However foolishly, we've put down roots in the shifting, sandy soil of the Edge of America. On summer afternoons, I sit on the back porch and watch dark skies build over James Island. Sometimes the storm pushes across the marsh; other days, it hits that humid wall of air and stops, leaving us lucky beach dwellers to flounder around in the surf with relatively little company on a gorgeous July day.

If there's a rule of Folly Beach living, it's not to complain about the heat. This is the very swelter that inspired DuBose Heyward and George Gershwin to pen the most subtly sweltering saunter in all of American music, *Summertime*. It's the air that both tortured and nourished quarantined sailors and weary soldiers during the Civil War. Their blood is still in the sand.

And it's the air I wake up each morning and breath, here from the porch looking out to the Folly River, as pelicans fly overhead and painted buntings dart between the sprawling live oaks that dot the yard.

It's the air I call home, and it's where I'm from.

**Stratton Lawrence**
Writer and Author, *Images of America Folly Beach*

Photo by Hunter McRae

*Morris Light Wave. Photo by Jonathan Jackson*

# Legacy of Valor

With its cobblestone streets and colorful row houses, with their sometimes-sagging, often elegantly restored piazzas, it's almost impossible to think of Charleston without recognizing its celebrated history. Many important dates crowd the city's rich historical timeline, but featured prominently is December 20, 1842—the date that the South Carolina legislature voted to establish The Citadel.

The Citadel is a small, scenic campus that sits on the banks of the Ashley River. The focal point of campus is Summerall Field, the parade ground where the Friday afternoon dress parades take place. Along the perimeter of the parade ground are administrative and academic buildings, as well as five battalions—white stucco fortress-like barracks where the cadets reside.

Like the cadets who first arrived in 1843, I reported to The Citadel in 1969 for a college education and military training. Unlike those cadets, however, I had been recruited to play football. Round trip airfare from Jacksonville, Florida, where my parents lived, to Charleston back then was $30. I lived in Murray Barracks. There was no air conditioning, and from the open windows wafted in the pungent smell of pluff mud. But the pluff mud didn't compare to the overwhelming smell of sulfur from the paper mill in North Charleston that assaulted us when the wind blew our way on overcast days. Throughout the year, the Westminster chimes sounded from the bell tower on the quarter hour, and in the spring, honeysuckle filled the air.

Braving life as a freshman cadet was not for the faint of heart, as I quickly learned. I remember returning from football practice and asking my roommate why we chose to live such a regimented existence in Spartan-like quarters, when we could instead be managing our own time and living a far more comfortable life in any other college dorm in America. Then and there, we decided to quit, but we would wait until after parents' weekend.

Parents' weekend, though, turned into Thanksgiving furlough, then Christmas, and then spring break. For some reason, which escaped us at the time, we kept coming back. We took life one day at a time. The days turned into weeks and the weeks into months, and somewhere in the midst of the constant drilling, the endless marching, the saluting, my classmates and I realized that we had become part of something much larger than ourselves or our own education—we shared a bond that intrinsically tied us to one another and kept us going.

Two other events during my cadet years would shape my life: when I was a sophomore, I met Donna Kangeter, a Charleston native, and when I was a junior, I had a chance, but life-changing conversation with an Air Force ROTC instructor one afternoon as I was coming off the football field.

After four eventful years in Charleston, it was time to graduate and begin the next chapter of my life. Donna and I married in Summerall Chapel in the weeks following graduation, and thanks to the Air Force instructor's sage advice, I commissioned in the Air Force and began a 32-year career. During those years, Donna and I lived at 24 different addresses spanning the globe—Alabama, Florida, Georgia, Hawaii, Idaho, Kansas, Korea, New Mexico, Scotland, South Carolina, and Washington, D.C. We had two sons, Jonathan and Brad, and eventually a daughter-in-law, Elisha, and two grandsons—Michael and Matthew.

In January 2006, we moved back to Charleston, where it all began and where our roots lay. It was finally time to settle down.

Now, as I look at the bright faces of the 2,300 young men and women who march by me in their gray wool uniforms at Friday afternoon parades, I am reminded that their time in Charleston and at The Citadel is shaping their destinies, too. On the east side of the parade ground, behind the parading cadets, sits Summerall Chapel—profound and majestic. An inscription on the

front of the chapel reads, "Remember now thy Creator in the days of thy youth." Also inscribed are the names of the scores of Citadel alumni who have given their lives in defense of our country—at once a solemn reminder of and an homage to their sacrifice. The Citadel's legacy of graduates—who have fought in every American war since the Mexican War—began well before we were born, and it will continue long after we die. This legacy, like Fort Moultrie and Fort Sumter, is a part of Charleston's deep history that lives with us still today, palpable around us everywhere as we walk the city's narrow cobblestoned streets. There's a battle rhythm to life here at The Citadel that draws us in and makes us part of this great family of patriot leaders.

What does Charleston mean to me? It means The Citadel. It means patriotism. It means family.

Charleston means home.

**Lt. Gen. John W. Rosa, USAF (Ret.)**
President, The Citadel

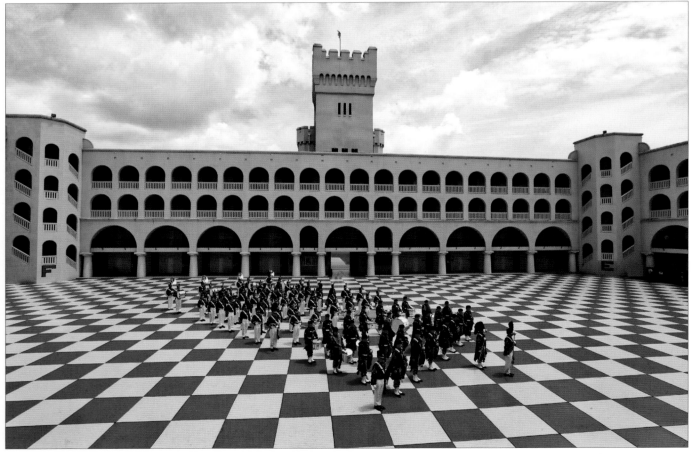

*Photos courtesy of Russ Pace, The Citadel*

# Fair Winds and Following Seas

I can't think of anywhere in the world I would rather live, raise a family, and work than Charleston. I was born here, to the most wonderful parents a child could dream of. My parents taught me how to appreciate this magical city, and my father introduced me to the Lowcountry outdoors at an early age. Our fishing and hunting adventures became unforgettable treasures.

My father was one of the pioneers of the offshore fishing grounds off Charleston in the mid sixties. In those early days we fished in small boats, with antiquated electronics. We would run 60 miles offshore in a 20-foot Bertram with nothing more than an AM radio to help us find our way home.

My dad introduced me to Marlin tournament fishing in the early seventies. The old Charleston Yacht Club is my first memory of tournament fishing. There was nothing more exciting to a young teenager than to watch the boats come in and unload and weigh their catches. The old Charleston City Marina was located where the Charleston Megadock is located today.

The South Carolina Governor's Cup Billfish Series began in the early 2000s and has continued to grow. The series attracts anglers from all over, and these anglers have come to enjoy not only our great fishing, but also Charleston's well-known Southern hospitality and its great food. Charleston is usually the favorite stop for boat owners and captains traveling our coast.

My introduction to fishing at an early age was the reason I chose my career as a sportfishing boat captain. I graduated from Clemson University with a degree in Industrial Management, but I knew what I wanted to do with my life. I didn't know how, but I knew I wanted to go home to Charleston and start fishing for a living. I got my break, found my dream boat, and began charter fishing out of Bohicket Marina. Since those early days, I have experienced some wonderful fishing, with several tournament wins, but the best thing was meeting some great people who influenced my life's direction.

The offshore fishing season began in April and ran through September. During the rest of the year, we would fish for red drum, trout, and flounder. Charleston's inshore fishing is world-renowned.

Partly because of these experiences, I was able to travel and fish other exotic destinations throughout the Caribbean. I captained the *Sportin' Life* for the Eubank family for almost 20 years. What a great family! I will always be indebted to the Eubanks for the opportunities they offered me. The hailing port on the *Sportin' Life* was, of course, Charleston, South Carolina.

There were countless occasions in our travels where people would stop and say hello and make the comment that Charleston was their favorite city. I have always felt truly blessed to live and work in Charleston. I have been offered opportunities to move and fish elsewhere, but I never wanted to leave the Lowcountry.

Hopefully we will cross paths in this wonderful town, and if you meet me on the boat I captain, I promise you the hailing port will be Charleston, South Carolina. *Tight lines!*

**Captain Mike Glaesner**
Captain of Sportfish boat *Ultra* and Drumbeat Charters and member, G. Loomis and Kaenon Pro Staffs

Photo by Rhonda Glaesner

*Patriots Point, on the Charleston Harbor in Mount Pleasant, SC, is the home of Patriots Point Naval and Maritime Museum and a fleet of National Historic Landmark ships, including the USS YORKTOWN, Cold War Memorial and the only Vietnam Support Base Camp in the U.S. Patriots Point is also headquarters to the Congressional Medal of Honor Society and the agency's official Medal of Honor Museum. Photo by Beki Reynolds*

*Fort Sumter is notable for two battles of the American Civil War. It was one of a number of forts planned after the War of 1812, combining high walls and heavy masonry. Work started in 1829, but was incomplete by 1860, when South Carolina seceded from the Union. The First Battle of Fort Sumter opened on April 12, 1861, when Confederate artillery fired on the Union garrison. These were the first shots of the war, and continued all day, watched by many civilians in a celebratory spirit. The fort had been cut off from its supply line, and surrendered the next day. The Second Battle of Fort Sumter, September 8, 1863, was a failed attempt by the Union to re-take the fort, dogged by rivalry between army and navy commanders. Although the fort was reduced to rubble, it remained in Confederate hands until it was evacuated as Sherman marched through South Carolina in February 1865. Fort Sumter is now a National Monument with a Visitor Education Center. Photo by Martha Lawrence*

*Ravenel Bridge at Night. Photo by Steven Hyatt*

# College Pride

The College of Charleston has been an important part of my life for 46 years. Since 1969, I've been coming to this campus in downtown Charleston. I've seen the college grow from a small private college of about 425 students to its present public, mid-major status of more than 11,000 students. I've worked for seven distinguished men who served as its President.

I chose to come to the College of Charleston because of three factors: (a) it was going to be an academic challenge for me, (b) I wanted to be a part of the challenge of integrating the College of Charleston and (c) as an athlete, I did not have to re-establish myself with the local sports media. To this day, if I had to do it again, the decision would be the same. I'm very fortunate to be a part of the history of the college, particularly for my place in integrating the college and my role in its athletics department.

Upon my arrival to the campus, there was no doubt that I was a minority in a totally white environment. There was little there for me to identify with other than my teammates. Classes were no different; I was the only black in many of my classes and often times got passed over during class discussions. It was clear in my mind that some professors preferred that I not be there. But my years at Moultrie High had prepared me for this.

I often say that those of us who were here in the late sixties and early seventies are pioneers who paved the way for what you now see at the College of Charleston in terms of black faces on campus. These black faces will never go through some of what we went through.

The College has launched a diversity initiative that addresses all minorities under one umbrella. But, when I think of minorities and the college, I think of black faces. In reality, the college still has a long way to go with regard to bringing racial balance in the areas of administration, faculty, and students. The only area at the college where you have a large visible amount of blacks is in janitorial, cafeteria, and grounds services, all of which may be viewed as low paying jobs.

Nonetheless, I'm very proud to have been a part of the movement to integrate the College, and I would like to thank three individuals who are very special to me. First, thanks to the late Mr. Theodore Stern, the sixteenth president of the College, for his great leadership during a most difficult time for the College of Charleston. Very special thanks to my friend and mentor of 46 years, Mr. Frederick Daniels, who at the time was the Director of Admissions and Head Men's Basketball Coach, for recruiting and bringing me to the College.

Finally, I would thank my mother who is no longer with us, but lives within my heart every day. It was her words of encouragement that got me through all those encounters at Moultrie High and the College. She always taught me to treat people the way I wanted to be treated, to speak to people the way I wanted to be spoken to, and above all to have manners. It all boils down to respecting your fellow man.

**Otto B. German**
Assistant Director of Athletics/Compliance and second black athlete to graduate at College of Charleston, Class of 1973

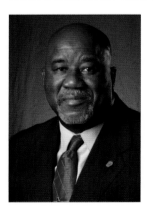

*Cistern Theater, College of Charleston, South Carolina. Photo by Eric Horan*

*Shem Creek. Photo by Paul Andrew Dunker*

# Preserving Community

The waters surrounding Charleston's peninsula and its remarkable barrier islands are my refuge, and they're also how I make my living. I've been a flats fishing guide for two decades, and I've seen the industry grow exponentially in recent years. When I started in 1994, I was one of five or six inshore guides. Now, over 150 professional guides take to the water daily to give visitors a glimpse of the Lowcountry angling life.

The salt marsh is the heartbeat of our ecosystem, and the creeks are the arteries by which all estuarine life subsists, within the ever-changing boundaries of the spartina grass. The evolution of the coastal landscape is paralleled by Charleston's progressive era of development. Right now we are experiencing a time of unprecedented growth for our beloved city. Nature will always select its own course, but can we prosper while also protecting that which sustains us?

Yes, a lot has changed since the world found us. And it's okay. I'm one of many who welcome progress; it would be unrealistic to think everything will always remain the same. We have to adapt and embrace change, but we should maintain that which beckons people to come here in the first place.

I support conservation organizations that provide a voice to protect special places with specific regard to a healthy economy. Without them, we stand to lose the surroundings that made Charleston what it is, to greed, money and politics. Other local nonprofit groups work incessantly to preserve the character of the city itself. Can you paint your house any color you want in the historic district or replace a slate roof with shingles? Can you replace old heart pine siding with HardiPlank? Can you build a high rise office tower downtown? No, you can't, at least not without proper approval. And that's a good thing, it's why Charleston still has the feel and integrity of a colonial city hundreds of years old. All of these causes contribute to a well-preserved, exceptional quality of life, and more and more large companies have established a presence because of what the area has to offer. Businesses that make efforts to help maintain Charleston's natural and historical significance become examples for the type of industry the area wants.

Charleston has long been a place of interest to the rest of the world in one way or another. My ancestors came here many generations ago, and I want future generations to be able to appreciate everything I've been able to enjoy: cast netting for shrimp, fly fishing for tailing Redfish and hunting in old rice fields. Thus, I try to encourage respect for the environment and responsible planning for the future of this great place. I support legislation regarding limits and management of vulnerable species like spotted sea trout and Cobia. I am vocal in my community about issues that affect the quality of life here. I do this because Charleston is in my blood. I feel fortunate to have grown up here, and I care about what happens to it after I'm gone.

**Peter H. Brown**
Owner of Saltwater Charters, LLC

Photo by Kevin Jurgens

"A marsh hunt has a certain pace and sense about it. Even the horses and dogs seem to enjoy it more. Maybe it's the salt in the air."

— ELIZABETH SHER

*A Lowcountry Hunt. Photo by Elizabeth Sher*

Admiral's House. Photo by Amelia Weaver

# Going Away to Come Home

Raised in the wide-open, languid Mississippi Delta, with pages of expansive porches and miles of two-lane highways for meandering thoughts, I believed that words were a vehicle to see the world. As an English major, my Ole Miss education of bourbon-soaked conversations at the City Grocery bar in Oxford about the romantic lives of Ernest Hemingway's Havana and Walker Percy's New York City spurred me to seek out a definition of myself that seemed somehow bigger than my current surroundings in Mississippi would allow.

So I migrated to New York City to become a writer when an art gallery owner, and true Southern gentleman, Hollis Taggart spotted me in a vintage gold coat at one of his openings and hired me on the spot. More fodder for my writing, I thought. Years of hustle and ambition to learn the subtleties of art and the skills of the deal followed.

My Alabama-born mother Jacque called my twenties "an era of discernment and Yankee wandering." Nestled in my tiny, six floor walk-up, West Village apartment one night, inhaling the moon pies she shipped in bulk while the snow continued to fall, I could no longer deny that the unsettled chill looming in my bones was more than the unfriendly weather. It was time to go home. I shed New York City like an old coat.

I never intended to live in Charleston, but I am grateful for a God of providence. After fifteen years here, it would take the rapture or a raging hurricane to dislodge me. Had I become a writer, I do not think I would have had the same sense of place or longing to be in this land. The aging antebellum architecture, cool breeze off the water, and familiar conversational rhythms were and continue to be a salve to the Northern aggression. Walking the cobblestone streets was a homecoming to a newer version of me that realized home, and particularly Charleston, was perhaps the most romantic destination of all.

And then, the art. I was wholeheartedly seduced by the art of the South, and a pioneer in the Southern art market, Rob Hicklin, offered me an entirely new and intense level of education at his Charleston Renaissance Gallery in historic downtown Charleston. I poured over unsung masterpieces and researched an array of artists and their established or burgeoning markets. I was particularly intrigued by the modern artists and photographers who pushed beyond the traditional and explored controversial topics through progressive styles and mediums. Rob and I spent many afternoons debating the meaning of "Southern modern art" and how it translated into the market. We never came to an agreement, and I eventually turned in my gallery keys on a spring day as nearby St. Philip's rang noon-thirty.

I could not ignore the fact that a new Charleston was emerging in which contemporary did not only mean paintings of palmettos or rainbow row by living artists. Thousands of doodles on a legal pad, plus blood, sweat, and tears—and a generous supply of bourbon—became, over a decade ago, Rebekah Jacob Gallery. I seek out artists who stay true to their Southern roots—not by solely focusing on the beauty of the landscape, but also by exploring the complexities and conundrums of the place we call home.

The voices of my father, who encouraged entrepreneurship, and my mother, who encouraged the arts, intersect and echo in my mind as I foster, exhibit, broker, promote, and champion the artists I believe embody Southern Modern. Controversial subjects ignite me, and I continue to explore art works that deal with race, gender and sexuality. I believe in addressing

*Afterlife.* Photo by Sandy Dimke

the unspeakable through the visual with boldness and sophistication. Easy is overrated.

I have a particular affinity for documentary photography, whether vintage or contemporary, as it integrates a strong, intricate narrative to the visuals that extend where words end. My favorite WPA authors / photographers like Eudora Welty and Walker Evans traveled the Carolinas, photographing and writing about this land of elegant decay, still struggling to heal from the Civil War. Similarly, many contemporary photographers like Julia Cart and Richard Sexton poignantly capture and document fading structures and archetypal characters in a way that still entrances me.

I started out a writer, but through the visual arts, I found my voice. I had to go away to come home, to open my eyes—and put down the pen—in order to see.

**Rebekah Jacob**
Owner, Founder and Certified Appraiser, Rebekah Jacob Gallery

Photo by Jonathan Balliet

*Palmetto Roses and Sweetgrass Baskets. The sweetgrass basket making tradition came over with African slaves to America. From rice winnowing baskets to egg baskets, reeds and grasses were harvested, dried and woven into beautiful working containers. The Palmetto Rose, legend has it, was made by Southern women and given to their true, everlasting love. It is said that the rose would keep them safe from harm. Above; photo by Delk Haigler, left; photo by Beki Reynolds*

*John Cordes Prioleau House, 68 Meeting Street. Built in 1808, it was later owned by Dr. Charles Sheppard, who established Pinehurst Tea Plantation. William Bachman Chisolm updated the property in 1894. Photo by Martha Lawrence*

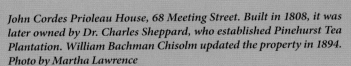

*The Four Corners of Law representing federal, state, local and ecclesiastical law on each corner of the intersection of Meeting and Broad Streets. Photos by Martha Lawrence.*

# Celebrate History and Diversity

Charleston is a place of storied history and culture. Tourists from around the world flock to the city to take in the sights from the Colonial and Antebellum years to the modern day. Charleston is a wonderful amalgam of diverse communities that reflect both the roots of the city and the progress of the present day.

Charleston is a city with an amazing ability to come together in times of urgency, as was done in the aftermath of Hurricane Hugo's devastating effects and in the aftermath of the horrific tragedy at Mother Emanuel African Methodist Episcopal Church. Charleston is—as a writer friend of mine recently said—a city where you can be warmly greeted on the streets and in shops and churches and told to "have a blessed day."

I love Charleston for what it is, but I also love Charleston for what it could be, for the storied history and culture of Charleston is more complex that it appears to be at first glance.

Tourists soaking in the history of the city are sometimes not privileged to hear the history of the slaves who built much of the city, who were artisans and craftsmen, and whose West African knowledge of how to grow rice made Charleston one of the richest cities in the original colonies. Cultural traditions of Gullah worship, shrimping, and basket weaving are sometimes not infused with the stories of those who fought for liberation in the Antebellum years and with those who pressed for equality in the mid-20th Century push for civil rights.

Charleston's wonderful amalgam of diverse communities is being slowly eroded by gentrification and by the increasing inability of diverse businesses to locate on the peninsula and reap the resultant financial rewards of doing so.

Charlestonians do come together in times of urgent need, but those who come together often retreat into their "comfort zones" when the urgent need passes.

Photo by Russ Pace, The Citadel

I love Charleston for what it is, but I'll keep kindly but firmly advocating for what Charleston can be when people of good will stay together, work together, and formulate and implement ways and means of celebrating the city's rich history and diversity in a way that elevates the quality of life for all citizens. We can then celebrate our past and build on a future that will make a great city even better.

**Rev. Joseph Darby**
Presiding Elder of the Beaufort District of the AME Church and First Vice President of the Charleston NAACP

*Cathedral Above. Photo by Jonathan Jackson*

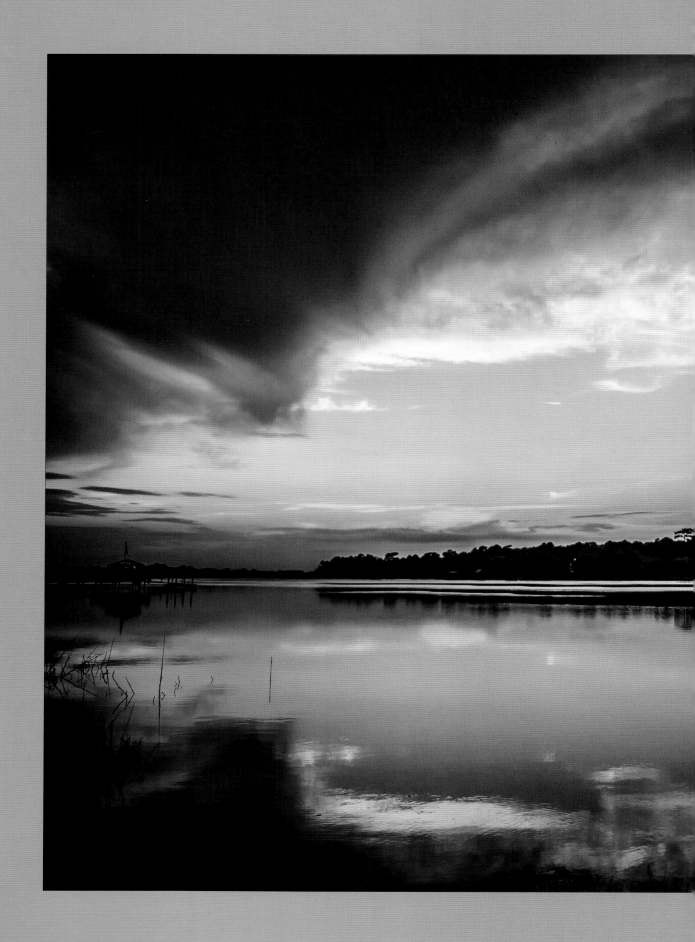

*Sunset. Photo by Michelle Bolton*

# A Painter's Paradise

My studio window is thrown wide open to King Street as I write, where the sound of a busker and her banjo competes with the clop, clop of a horse and carriage. The air is heavy with confederate jasmine. I am in a painter's paradise.

As a very green brown-eyed girl, I unpacked my bags on Gadsden Street forty-five years ago and have been engaged in a love affair with Charleston ever since. Gramling—a tiny South Carolina hamlet at the foot of the mountains—will always be where I am *from*. And Charleston will always be where I *became*—the place where my children were born.

As I'm fond of saying, if you don't mean to live here, don't linger. Charleston is one seductive town. She is painted often and painted well, so the challenge lies in interpreting this lush city and her inhabitants with one's own unique point of view. My friends and gallery owners, Joe and Janie Sylvan, say never walk down the street behind me as I am apt to come to a complete and abrupt halt. It's true. I turn a corner and am arrested by a peachy slice of light as it falls on some glorious texture, or on a clutch of basket makers as they weave, defining a one-time-only, delicious moment that holds me captive.

It has been my joy to literally grow up painting in Charleston with artists who have worked hard at getting better and at creating an atmosphere in which artists can support themselves. Now artists from all over flock here to paint and, seduced, stay.

Having painted here for so long, our stories are boundless. One flawless spring morning I was painting on South Battery, squinting, pacing, trying to capture the light, when a slightly strident voice "from off" asked, "Who told you that you could use those colors?" The smart aleck Southerner in me *had* to reply: "My Mama!"

An elitist, exclusive Charleston is not the Charleston I have known. On the contrary, I feel embraced. Of course, I haven't aspired to become a member of the St. Cecilia, or claimed to be named for anyone other than my Grandmother Rhett, a country doctor's wife in the Old English part of the state. Art is the loveliest possible common denominator, the language that blinds us to our differences. Or not. The juxtaposition of opposites that excites our eye in a painting may, with a broader brush, excite us as human beings.

From hastily sprayed graffiti to those patient white dots that are egrets, from King Street rattling to life at dawn to a marsh hush, from a down and dirty dive to the symphony, from a luminescent morning sky to sky reflected on shiny-wet cobblestones, from tea olive to pluff mud—I soak up every facet like the thirstiest sponge. And in some part magic/part hard work way, it comes out in the next painting, or the next painting or the next—the best painting always lying just around the bend.

From even the most exotic, far flung adventure, I come back happy, happy to return. When people ask, "Still painting?" I reply both laughingly and with sober reverence, "Take my pulse." I live it and I breathe it in this painter's paradise.

**Rhett Thurman**
Rhett Thurman's art may be seen in historic downtown Charleston at The Sylvan Gallery and her studio, where she works and lives with her husband, Harry Clark.

Photo by Harry Clark

*Nesting Egrets*

*Spoonbills over the Marsh. Photos by Kelley Luikey*

*Dixie Avenue. Photo by Jonathan Jackson*

"Life is a rolled-down window, a little cash from the ATM, a cold beer after a long sunburn. Life is a big grackle squawking in the live oak, an osprey whistling to her young, an owl answering a crow."

— DOUGLAS CUTTING

*Sentinels. Photo by Terry Knight*

# My Place, My Passion, My Tribe

As I reflect on Charleston, my thoughts are filled with the influences of my mother. In a city plagued with a history of slavery, she opened my eyes to the richness of African American culture.

Every Christmas we honor her tradition of reading *The Christmas Story, Gullah Edition*, which celebrates the roots of our Charleston heritage. She reads the Gullah version, and we take turns translating alongside her, and between giggles, we learn the value of this Lowcountry lineage.

I remember our Saturday morning outings to the King Street shopping district, where we would visit the city's retail staples: Anne's, Berlin's, Nancy's and Croghan's. These shopping escapades really planted the seed for who I would become.

Culture was key in my house as a child. I have such fond memories of attending MOJA events and walking through Marion Square for Spoleto festivities. Fast-forward to my own adulthood, and I am raising my son with my mother's fervor. I cherish the summers of watching him perform at SummerStage Theatre Camp at the historic Dock Street Theatre, where I saw countless plays and concerts, including Jump Little Children's annual Holiday rock show. How amazing that I would later use the same theatre as the backdrop for my own work shooting fashion editorials.

Thanks to my mother, I discovered my place in the art scene. I performed poetry regularly with the Poetic Jazz Society at the dynamic Avery Research Center, a museum of African American history, as well as the Jazz staple of the city, The Mezzane, the place where I fell in love with progressive jazz thanks to the band, Gradual Lean. Later I would have an art show of my own at the Old Cigar Factory, another Lowcountry landmark celebrating all of my life's experiences.

My big break career-wise came when I secured an opportunity to write a nightlife column for the *Charleston City Paper*, which gave me the chance to attend soirées, galas, and events around the city. All of my passions were colliding—art, fashion, music and people. I fell in love with something so valuable and something that has not been replicated in any other city I've known: COMMUNITY!

It's a beautiful thing how Charleston's community spirit works, and the creative community specifically is where I found my tribe! I learned the importance of relationships, a life lesson that contributes to my work and creativity. When my career began to grow and I found myself working as the fashion editor for *Charleston Magazine*, I thought about how fortunate I was to be able to do all of these things in my hometown. When I created Charleston Fashion Week, not only did my work place, *Charleston Magazine*, get behind it, but my beloved community rallied in support as well. In Charleston's fashion scene, now recognized worldwide, I became a pioneer in the creative community. I no longer live in Charleston, but I take it with me everywhere I go.

I miss cracking blue crabs with friends on the weekends or late night rendezvous at The Recovery Room, where, like Cheers, everyone knows your name. I miss the early morning recaps of the night before at Butcher & Bee and the many times my cohorts and I would pull together dance parties at The Faculty Lounge and The Royal American, and how it would be a wall-to-wall love fest brimming with diversity and unity. That's my city. Despite a history of division, a progressive community of thinkers, love warriors, creatives, and game changers evokes so much light in me. This love letter is my salute to them and the city. I am a reflection of you!

---

**Ayoka Lucas**
Stylist and Founder, Charleston Fashion Week and StylePublic.com

Photo by Corey Tenold Photography

*On the Runway, Charleston Fashion Week. Photo by Tim Sayer*

*Shem Creek. Photo by Marge Agin*

"There is something special about being in the waterways of the Lowcountry, surrounded by silence, except for the rustling of birds and the subtle sway of spartina grass."

— KEN BURGER

# A Place Like No Other

What is it about this place, this place called Charleston, this place we call home? What is it that makes us flock to this place like a swallow returning home to its chimney nightly? What makes us have a love affair with this pearl of a city located in a sea of pluff mud?

Is it the sea of oak and pine forests that surround our homes? Is it the almost unlimited exposure to rivers, creeks, and marshlands? The ebb and flow of the tide allows us to fill our body with those unusual smells from the seawaters and marshlands that are exposed and then covered on an irregular twelve-hour timetable.

Is it the immense historical footprint that Charleston made on our nation in the early years of formation in the 1600s and 1700s, or is it the climb to worldwide recognition that has taken place in the last thirty years that makes Charleston the envy of the South? Charleston is iconic and really no longer needs the state name to identify it.

Is it all of these things I mentioned, or is it just one of these things? To me, a man who has spent almost his entire life here, it is all of these things and more. It is the memories of childhood that wrap all of these elements into one sweet treasure chest of love for our home.

As a boy, I was fortunate enough to grow up on the peninsula of Charleston. Our home was three blocks from The Citadel and the marshes of the Ashley River, two blocks from Hampton Playground, three blocks from our elementary school, James Simons School, five blocks from Rivers High School, and luckily, right across the street from Hampton Park. This five-block semicircle provided me with endless adventures, entertainment, exercise, exploration in the marshes, and athletic events at the playground.

I can vividly recall hearing the sound of the morning bugle from the loudspeakers at The Citadel, waking their cadets and signaling the beginning of another day at the Military College of South Carolina.

The port city was a point of immigration for many of Europe's people yearning to be free from tyranny, dating back to the 1670s. As a result, we had a diverse cross-section of nationalities in our school: Greeks, Jews, Catholics and Protestants. I later learned that this was a very unusual trait for a Southern city. In high school, we became racially integrated with African Americans who lived close to our school. This exposure to many different cultures and religions was a wonderful learning experience. We learned about each other's religions by attending friends' church services on different Sundays. This is a practice we started in high school with our service club called the Key Club. It enlightened me in many ways and instilled an acceptance of religious difference. I later learned in college that this "Charleston practice of visiting other churches" was unique. I was again reminded that I came from a very special place in South Carolina and truly, a very special place in the South.

My grandfather moved with his family to Charleston in the early twentieth century. He had traveled the world employed by Standard Oil Company, known to most as ESSO. Having come from abject poverty, he educated himself and became a manager of ESSO's refinery in Havana, Cuba. Nearing retirement, he picked Charleston as his final work destination. He was enthralled with the natural splendor of Charleston, the rivers forming a deep-water port, the historical beauty, and the strong reverence for its history in the formation of this nation. As I heard him say many times, "Charleston is a special place—a gem waiting to be discovered—quite simply, it is a place like no other."

**Robert Lenhardt**
Businessman and Broad Street resident

Photo by Mary Ellen Lenhardt

*Unitarian Church and St. John's Lutheran Church Steeples. Photo by Amelia Weaver*

# Hospitality, the Heart and Soul of Charleston

In keeping with the tradition of generous reception in the Holy City, we are a family dedicated to hospitality. It's our business. It's Charleston's business. And like our great city, hospitality comes natural. We welcome people through our doors as we would welcome guests to our home. We shake hands and give hugs. We play music and entertain. We prepare elegant meals and pass plates with warmth and a gracious smile. No one is a stranger, and everyone is welcome.

We like to think of our kitchen as the heart of our business and the front of the house as its soul. The marriage of the two yields true Southern hospitality, the core of our mission and the spirit of our family. The truth is, we believe we're at our best when we're breaking bread together, sharing recipes and raising glasses. It's the Charleston way, and it's our way. And, there's always room at our table.

Photo by Michelle Bolton

**The Hall Family; Tommy, Jeanne, Bill, Sr. and Billy (not pictured)**
Proprietors, Hall's Chophouse, Slightly North of Broad, Rita's Seaside Grille, Old Village Post House and High Cotton

Photo by Martha Lawrence

*Drayton Hall's iconic portico is the only one of its kind in the world as it both projects from, and recedes into, the front of the house. Drayton Hall's portico was fully executed in the Palladian fashion, representing a sophisticated understanding of classical architecture. Drayton Hall was likely designed by John Drayton (d. 1779) and was completed in 1742. Located on the Ashley River about 15 miles northwest of Charleston, South Carolina and directly across the Ashley River from North Charleston. Photo by Eric Horan*

# Bringing the Movies Home

My life began with the sounds of gulls and halyards chiming against the masts and the pungent aroma of pluff mud emanating from the Charleston Yacht Basin, where my grandfather was undoubtedly tending to the latest of his hand-built boats.

It has been said many times that Charleston is where the Ashley and Cooper Rivers merge in Charleston Harbor to form the Atlantic Ocean. This may sound elitist, and it is, but to be from Charleston is to have a sense that one has entered this life in the center of the universe. One must travel to see all the wonders of the world, but Charleston is the greatest place to come back to.

The geography of Charleston is defined by its waterways, the pulse of rivers and creeks that rise and fall with the tides.

Imagine the long, perilous trip across the Atlantic Ocean by sail; imagine coming upon the sanctuary of such a great natural harbor, its rivers highways to the plantations, its creeks the streets of the Holy City. The city is indeed the peninsula between the Ashley and Cooper Rivers from the neck to the battery. But Charleston extends south to the Edisto Motel (formerly the home of the best fried seafood on the planet) east to the Santee Gun Club past the jetties, as far inland as Spanish moss grows, seaward to the black fish banks, and beyond to Europe.

I was blessed to cruise on the Holiday with my family on Charleston Harbor to view Fort Sumter and the Battery. We traveled up the rivers and through the rice fields to plantations and up the Intracoastal Waterway to all the barrier islands that dot the coast like a beautiful necklace. Sullivan's Island, Dewees, Capers and Bulls. Morris Island, Folly Beach, Johns Island, Kiawah, Seabrook, and Edisto.

The "Holy City" refers to the spires of countless churches and temples representing every faith. A divine sweet and salty mix of reverence and irreverence. Always with the bent elbow, like the tides, meals and libations are the rhythm of life. At social events a drink is an appendage. Food is the cornerstone of hospitality, a tradition that began with a pineapple stuck on wrought-iron gates. "Summertime and the living is easy, fish are jumpin' and the cotton is high." A patriotic rainbow of seafood: red fish, blue crabs, and white shrimp.

The bible is *Charleston Receipts*. The gospel includes the secrets to She-crab soup, red rice, fried chicken, and shrimp. If I were asked to describe Charleston in only two words it would be "fried shrimp."

My earliest memories include crossing the giant erector set known as the Cooper River Bridge, Easter in Hampton Park, and countless hours spent in the Charleston Museum on Rutledge Avenue. Beyond the huge white columns was an entire world of adventure. Indeed, you did not need to leave

Charleston to visit the mysteries of Egypt or travel in time to the age of dinosaurs.

King Street was lined with grand cinemas including The Gloria, Riviera, Garden, and America. Everyone dressed to the nines to attend, ushers in regal uniforms, lobbies of marble and brass. My dad introduced me to a world where one could close their eyes, and from the darkness, be magically transported to any place or time—Tarzan's jungle, Sinbad's ship or the Alamo.

This was my first glimpse into a world that would become my dharma, my life's work.

I studied history, art, photography and film but had a singular dream to live on Sullivan's Island and surf and sail as much as possible while pursuing my career. I found this at Porpoise Point in "Moultrieville." With a perch like that I had no reason to leave and became determined to make Charleston the greatest place in the world to shoot movies.

Hollywood began shooting more and more on location and I was given my introduction to feature films by working in the locations department of Wes Craven's cult classic *The Swamp Thing*, where I met many other young folks from South Carolina about to embark on film careers. We shot at Magnolia Plantation and Cypress Gardens, Fairfield Plantation, Hibernian Hall and the batteries of Sullivan's Island.

This was followed immediately by Paramount Pictures' adaptation of the Pat Conroy novel, *Lords of Discipline*, and I became one of South Carolina's first motion picture location managers. As a location scout and location manager, I have spent a lifetime bringing movies to shoot in South Carolina and assuring the film experience is a terrific one for all concerned.

As a location scout I have been able to make a living doing what I love, exploring every inch of America's most historic city and the surrounding villages and wilderness. I partake in the world's greatest hospitality, entering the grandest of Charleston single houses to the smallest of freeman's homes. I've climbed to the top of the steeples and into the dungeons, entered secret garden gates and lounged on verandas with spectacular views of the harbor. We have transported the length of Broad Street to war-torn ruins during the funeral of the Hunley crew. Upper King Street has been converted to the 1940s for *The Notebook*. Camera in hand, always making note of Charleston's unique details of light, patterns and texture … shadows through wrought iron gates, irregular sidewalk slate, cobble and ballast stones, grand oaks and palmetto trees.

Blessed with life's little extras, Charleston is my home.

---

**Steve Rhea**
Steve Rhea is a Charleston based film professional that has brought dozens of movies to the Palmetto State. With an artist's eye and a caring heart, he shares the beauty of his beloved home—Charleston.

*Charleston Waterfront. Photo by Martha Lawrence*

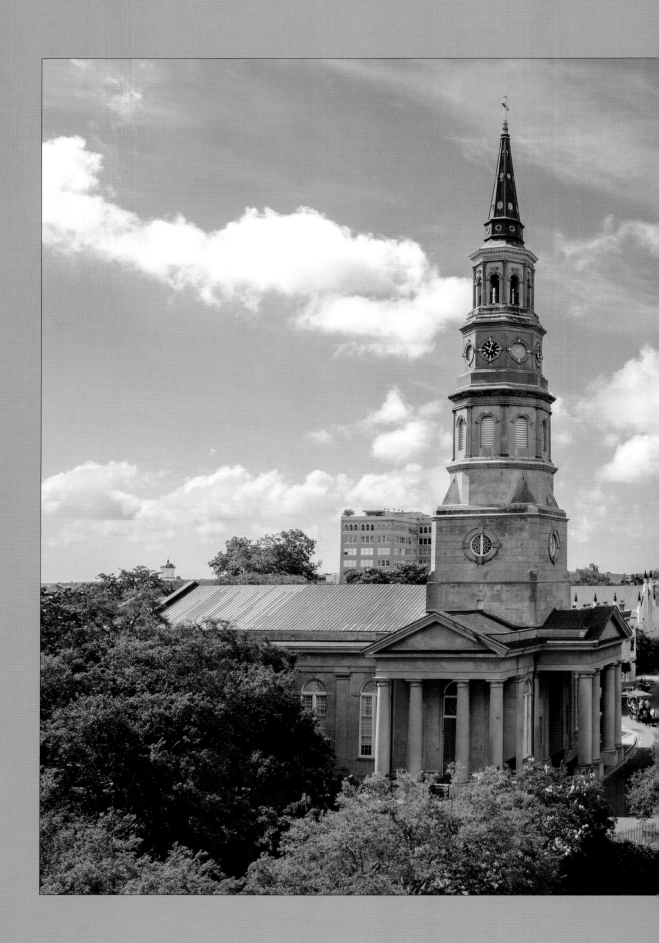

*St. Philip's Church. Photo by Steven Hyatt*

*Pitt St. Bridge Refined. Photo by Amelia Weaver*

# Pluff Mud and Kindness

My life in the Lowcountry has been a wondrous mix of aristocracy and good old tomboy fun. From being a pluff mud girl with that beautiful green goo between my toes, to making my debut among some of the most elite daughters of Charleston society—what a ride it's been.

*Charleston Blue Crabs.* Photo by Libby Williams

Lowcountry life called me from a very young age. The knowledge that I didn't become Southern, but was born Southern, was not lost on me. I had the best of both worlds when it came to being privileged and just like everybody else. I knew from a very young age that I could be, and do, both. And I did.

What defines all of us is our heritage. We must embrace it and live it to what suits our lives.

Afternoon ladies teas with my grandmother at the Carolina Yacht Club or afternoons at the Charleston Country Club pool while my grandparents played golf, helped mold me. The mandatory cotillion dancing lessons with Mrs. Whipple. All these things made me, me.

But so did wonderful days in Shem Creek, immersing myself in the salt water that runs through my veins.

By God's grace I have found a life of pure joy and I have found it in the wonders of my ancestors. I have found it in the life my parents provided for me.

My great-great grandfather developed the battery into the real estate wonder it is today. My grandmother was born in her home along with her sisters who lived just behind him on South Battery. What a joy to learn these things as a child growing up.

But the Lowcountry and Charleston is so much more than that. It's being on a John boat and finding any creek your boat can meander through. It's learning to pass by that beautiful waterfront wharf we call The Battery without saying a word about how it came to be, and watching people look on and admire it. It's humbleness and graciousness and manners that are not forced.

It's learning to throw a cast net properly and how to clean crabs—the right way.

Charleston is so many things to me. Its grandeur is amazing. Dress me up, and expect nothing but sophistication. Proper comes natural to me. But so does a suntanned body, bare feet—and perhaps the occasional sunburn. Cold beers, coozies, oysters and the like are Charleston staples.

In Charleston, coming from "somebody" doesn't make you somebody. You have to go out and make your own. Respect your elders and all those around you. Love hard. Be honest. Use good manners. But you must always do it with grace and dignity so that when you come into your own, you are your own person.

Most importantly, be kind. Kindness, which our beautiful Charleston is revered for, is so darn easy to do!

---

**Sully Witte**
Editor, *The Moultrie News*

*Pineapple Fountain at Night. Photo by Steven Hyatt*

# A Match Made in Heaven

I have spent my life in cities all over Africa and the East Coast, but now Charleston is my beloved home, and I never want to leave. I couldn't find a better city anywhere to found my school, the Charleston Academy of Domestic Pursuits. My passions are domestic architecture, entertaining and food, the DNA of Charleston. The city and I are a match made in heaven.

Charleston is the center of gracious hospitality in America, a characteristic rooted in its domestic architecture, scaled down for home living. Architecture informs the personality of many American cities. Chicago is the home of the modern skyscraper. New York is about what goes on outside of the home, at any hour of the day or night; even close friends might never see the inside of the other's apartment.

Charleston's porches and double porches have long been synonymous with hospitality. The porch is open to everyone and anyone, a place for family and friends to pass the time. They are often regarded as more important than the interior rooms. The temperate climate, and yearlong ease of access to the outdoors, offers a type of entertainment not available in many urban environments. Many historic houses have palatial, well-manicured gardens, essentially outdoor rooms used for all manner of hospitality. A five o'clock invitation frequently means dress for the weather and join us for a drink on our porch or in our garden.

Food is a major attraction; every week another outstanding restaurant opens its doors. Home cooks are serious too, ancient domestic pursuit skills have not receded so far into Charleston's past. Our seasons are known as deer, dove, duck and turkey; hosts polish heirloom sterling cups and prepare family recipes when giving cocktail parties; a few lucky residents own second floor ballrooms and are savvy enough to use these magnificent rooms for their intended purpose. Charleston is not the city to find an eighteenth century ballroom refitted into a home office or rec center.

Charleston has been a major port since Colonial times, which continues to give the city its sophisticated, international feel. Since the spice trade of the 1700s Charleston has adapted to different cultures and customs, which makes for an eclectic group of residents.

What the Charleston Academy of Domestic Pursuits espouses is what Charleston's residents have always known: a house is the ultimate tool for living. The city's character is the plinth atop which the Charleston Academy perches.

---

**Suzanne Pollak**
Founder of Charleston Academy of Domestic Pursuits and Author, *Entertaining for Dummies, The Pat Conroy Cookbook* and *The Charleston Academy of Domestic Pursuits Etiquette with Recipes*

*Charleston's gracious homes with their expansive porches are heralded for their beauty, elegance and style.*
*Photos by Martha Lawrence*

The Arthur Ravenel Jr. Bridge is a cable-stayed bridge over the Cooper River, connecting downtown Charleston to Mount Pleasant. Photo by Eric Horan

"Charleston has always been rooted in commerce, with prominent shipping terminals and a robust hospitality industry.

Today's Charleston draws entrepreneurs from across the country who want to live and work in a city steeped in both history and innovation."

— MINDY TAYLOR, Director of Growth and Opportunities, Qonceptual

# Romance of the Soul

I had lived in Charleston for almost a decade when I met John Doyle. I had several careers while finding my place in this city I still proudly call home after 20 years. John and the art community as a whole were off my radar that first 10 years, which is strange to think about now since the last decade of my life has been spent working for The John C. Doyle Art Gallery in the heart of our vibrant and growing French Quarter art district. The French Quarter holds a very special charm all of its own, and John loved every historic inch of it.

I will always treasure our countless discussions sitting in the natural light of the gallery, covering topics from the old King Street shops like Kerrisons that he loved as a child, to visiting Folly Beach in the 1950s and watching his parents dance on the promenade.

I learned more from John about the Charleston peninsula and surrounding islands in 10 years than I'll ever learn from any book. John became my close friend and confidant, and for that I am a very lucky woman.

John's first Charleston memories were the colorful wooden crates the Gullah vendors used to hold their vegetables and fruits at the corner of Broad Street and Meeting Street, and even as young as 3 or 4—John was intensely attracted to the color, and the light on the colors. He constantly sketched during church throughout his entire childhood, to his mother's chagrin! He treasured fishing with his father all around the Charleston harbor and barrier islands from Johns Island to Folly Beach, often catching the family dinner for the night, such as fresh mackerel. He told me of dogs sleeping in the streets, clotheslines across Church Street from tenement to tenement and the sound of the distant Gullah ice man singing his offerings up and down the street. John didn't have to 'make up' a romantic setting to grow up in. He said on many occasions that the gods gifted Charleston to him in that

Battery Park. Photo by John Carroll Doyle

way, and the sole purpose was for him to be an artist.

John spent a great deal of time as a young man by Colonial Lake, which is nestled between Ashley Avenue and Rutledge Avenue, just one block from his humble home at 12 Trumbo Street. He often told me the lake was "just like the Atlantic in its possibilities!" He was basically allowed to roam free in the 1940s and '50s when parents had little fear of harm coming to their gallivanting kids. I learned from John that the present day market area, full of shops and tourists, was originally called the "blood bucket," and he was not allowed to *ever* go there, though of course he did!

Many paintings from his career that spanned over 40 years were inspired by real experiences he had in that area as a child, or in the least observed in that vicinity of sailors, brothels, and depravity.

As John got older, Charleston remained a sleepy town, but that changed with Hurricane Hugo in 1989. John was working hard as an aspiring artist, and newly sober from drugs and alcohol—which fueled his creativity and lust for life in ways he never imagined. His sobriety brought him a "new Charleston" as he would say to me, one where he understood that his status in the community was based on action and integrity, and not the poor and humble beginnings that caused him to doubt himself for so many years.

Post-Hugo Charleston brought a slow but steady revitalization to all parts of Charleston, and John's dedication and hard work paid off as he enjoyed many successes once the town began to see more tourists that loved his art depicting romantic Charleston. His sales were booming, both with locals that knew the direct reflection of Charleston in his art, and especially visitors that wanted to take home a "piece" of Charleston.

He remained most of his 71 years on the historic Charleston peninsula, and he became an iconic figure to be seen walking

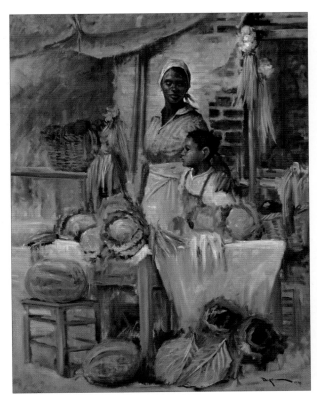

*Oil paintings by John Carroll Doyle*

on the streets in his all black attire, always walking with purpose and vitality.

I think the most important thing I learned from John Doyle about the true nature of Charleston is that it really is a kind and prolifically beautiful place to live if you have the right eyes to see it. Beauty is everywhere, all the time … in the lavender shadows John painted so delicately, in the sway of a palm that may have been here since John as a child played alongside Colonial Lake dreaming about his future. Although John and I were planning a few trips before his passing in November 2014, he said to me quite often "Angie, *Charleston is my Italy*, why do I need to go anywhere?"

I think the answer to this question lies in the thousands of paintings John created reflecting the beauty and history of unique Charleston, and thankfully because of his prolific talent—local Charleston collectors, as well as ones around the world are reminded of our beloved city every time they pause to see the stories of Charleston reflected in their paintings, as well as a little bit of the soul of John himself. Johns always said that "art is more about the artistic soul of the artist than the subject."

**Angela Stump**
Gallery Director, The John Carroll Doyle Art Gallery
In Memoriam: John Carroll Doyle
December 22, 1942 - November 12, 2014

*Clockwise from top left: Ironworked gate bids welcome; A Heron perches in a cypress tree in the Audubon Swamp; slaves' cabins.*

*Photos by Karen Peluso*

Founded in 1676 by the Drayton family, Magnolia Plantation has witnessed the history of our nation unfolding from the American Revolution through the Civil War and beyond. It is the oldest public tourist site in the Lowcountry and the oldest public gardens in America, opening its doors to visitors in 1870. Magnolia Plantation and Gardens is Charleston's most visited plantation.

Clockwise from top left: The path up from the Ashley River; the Biblical Garden; Live oak and the gardener's cottage.

Circular Flood. Photo by Jonathan Jackson

# As the Tide Rises, We Unite

Sometimes it takes a disaster to realize what is important in our lives. In September 1989, Charlestonians experienced Hurricane Hugo. It devastated everyone. But through the devastation, the "Holy City" lived up to her name. We were all one big family bonding together to help, to share and to love our neighbors. I remember feeling God's presence as our city united and began to put the pieces back together to make Charleston stronger and better than ever.

It has been decades since the eye of Hugo glared upon us, and I am just as proud of Charlestonians now as I've ever been with their response to disaster. During the Johns Island tornado, homes and properties were completely destroyed. As the clean-up began, the people came, just as they had after Hugo. Strangers and friends came together with chain saws, rakes, food, water, and their willingness to help. They gave up their time, their money, and their hearts to help those in need.

After the Mother Emanuel tragedy, the world saw firsthand how we remained united during a time of unspeakable grief. We walked forward as one and refused to let such a horrific act of hate tear us apart. We embraced each other like never before and made sure we told our loved ones, our neighbors, our teachers, our grocers how much we cared for them. June 17, 2015 woke us up to the frightening disparity that still exists in this world. In the days and weeks that followed, Charlestonians chose harmony over frenzy to remember and pay our respect to the nine lives lost and the victims that survived.

And during the 1000-year flood caused by torrential downfalls of rain, people came with their pants rolled up and water boots on, ready to help. The people of Charleston bond together in times of distress, and in those times, we shine as a beacon of hope to the rest of the country.

So when I am asked why I love Charleston, the Holy City, I can only respond with a simple statement: I feel God's presence in the people here.

He is in the hearts of all those who love this beautiful city, those who have a deep faith that leads them to follow the greatest commandment, to "Love the Lord thy God with all thy heart, with all thy soul, with all thy mind … and to love their neighbor as themselves."

We are all neighbors, from Johns Island to Sullivan's Island, from the Peninsula to Awendaw, from River Road to Remount Road. And that's what makes Charleston such a special place.

**Pam Morris Hanckel**
Treasurer at Hanckel Marine and
Author, *GRITS: God Reigns in the South*

*Vivid. Photo by Marge Agin*

# Harvesting Doughnuts

When I close my eyes and think of my childhood as I grew up on Johns Island, I smell sweet corn growing in the fields, the same fields that I played hide and go seek in with my brother, my sister and my cousins who lived down the dirt road. I think of my sweet nanny, Tina, who loved me like her own, and I hear her singing me the most beautiful lullabies in her native Gullah tongue. I think of rosy red tomatoes growing on the vine. I remember the way they smelled too, especially at the end of the season. That rotten smell simply never leaves me. I think of my family of five living in a 900 square foot house that had more love than any mansion you could think of. I long to scream, "MOMMA!!! The cows are in the yard again."

I think about seeing fresh caught blue crabs crawling out of the pot of boiling water, and I can see them running all over the kitchen floor and everyone scrambling to get them back into the pot. I smell the glorious pluff mud that we use to roll in, sink in and play in until we even had it in our teeth. I think of the farm workers cutting ripe, juicy watermelons in the fields and eating them as it dripped off my chin down my beautiful and crisp smocked dress. I feel the salt water envelope me as I jumped off my cousins' dock and floated down the beautiful Abbapoola Creek to my great-grandparents' dock, or vice versa depending on which way our magical creek was flowing. I feel my just right sun-kissed skin after endless days playing outside.

I can taste the delicious tea and homemade cookies that "Cuddin Lila" would serve my cousin and me every time we knocked on her door. She'd happily serve us on her most exquisite china, the "good stuff," with not a care that we were clumsy little girls. I think of nights when we laid in the Lowcountry grass staring up at the big, beautiful Carolina moon in all of its majesty. I think of the first fish I caught and how proud everyone was of that tiny fish, like it was a trophy. I hear my Momma telling my cousin and me tales of Brer Rabbit in the best Uncle Remus voice ever.

I cherish my childhood and how blessed I was to grow up in a simpler time and place. I would give anything to go back to my idyllic childhood. There's just one thing that I never seem to find—the doughnuts that my Momma always talked about people cutting as we were leaving Jenkins Farm Road. I knew where the corn, tomatoes, cucumbers, soybeans, watermelon and cantaloupe grew. I just never found the doughnuts that everybody cut.

**Amy Jenkins Beckum**
Johns Island native

*Solitude. Photo by Sandy Dimke*

# Along Saltwater Lines

After living a nomadic existence for eight years, Teresa and I looked for a spot to grow our roots, and the Lowcountry called. We have lived and played from the Florida Everglades to the rivers of Alaska and can't ask for more from our adopted home. Salt water seems to be one of the lines that connect our favorite places together, and when deciding on a place to plant ourselves, Charleston was at the top of the list.

The South is alluring with its bountiful forests, starry sultry nights, and if you live on the coast as we do, offerings from the ocean can sustain a body and soul. Salt air permeates the Lowcountry like the smell of shrimp and grits in a small kitchen. When you're here, it becomes a part of you, and this is the foundation of the flavor of Charleston. Incidentally, that same salty taste also called to us in a primal way and became the essence of our business—making Southern culinary sea salt.

Shortly after settling into our new home, we hosted a quintessentially Southern hog roast. Southerners are serious about their BBQ, and we made quick friends within our community. Feeling comfortable with a laid back party, we made the event a potluck and asked everyone to bring a side dish and a chair. We brined our hog with seawater and boiled a few gallons down to collect the salt from the water. As the hog smoked on the grill, our dish of salt sat right next to it, and, like the hog, took on the color of brown sugar, becoming the talk of the party. We were encouraged by our delighted guests and the realization that there wasn't anyone harvesting sea salt within a thousand miles of us, and our new business was born.

The camaraderie between the local business owners in the Charleston area is invaluable and we have found a supporting network of like-minded "makers" to collaborate with. These relationships are built on a free exchange of advice and genuine friendship that is a marvel of the Southern business world. Collaborations like these are just an extension of Charleston hospitality, which is also helping other local artisans get their wares out to the rest of the country.

Charlestonians are genuinely some of the kindest people we have ever had the pleasure of knowing. This is a place where the pace is slower and the smiles and casual conversations are more frequent. It is here where you can walk down the cobblestone streets, buy a rose for your lover, watch the dolphins feed from the pier, and stroll past jubilant brides and grooms, bicyclists and sweetgrass baskets; and all the while, of course, you can always taste the salt in the air.

**Rustin and Teresa Gooden**
Bulls Bay Saltworks

Photo by Lindsey Harris

Photo by Rinne Allen

*Above, a baby Loggerhead Turtle makes its first trip into the sea. Below, a Mobula Ray breaks through the surface of the water.*
*Photos by Kelley Luikey*

# The Knowing Nose

Introspection at Middleton Place. Photo by Sandy Dimke

Charleston, how do I love thee? Let me smell the ways. I think the first time I realized that Charleston could be identified by olfactory sense alone was on a hot July day exiting a CHS flight a few years back. In two seconds flat my hair curled (frizzed) and I was both assaulted and welcomed to the Lowcountry by a combination of wet earth and wafting paper mill. I don't think there is a soul around here who hasn't giggled and accused a car rider of flatulence because of this combination of smells. Home sweet home.

Of the many cities in the six states that I have lived, I don't think any are as recognizable by scent as Charleston! A few examples:

Pluff Mud. That tidal brown thick residue that's left after the tide goes out; it can suck even the best-tied shoe off your foot. Its heady, salty aroma may be the first to greet you at any non-beach shoreline.

Suntan Lotion. At the end of every public beach path lie hundreds of bodies slathered in potions. Coastal breezes greet us with the identifiable bouquet of coconut and medicinal UVA protection. This smell is a huge blessing considering what hundreds of bodies sweltering in the sun and Charleston humidity *should* smell like!

Boiled Peanuts. I am not sure who the first person to boil a peanut was, or why they did so, but they should have an honorary statue near John C. Calhoun in Marion Square Park.

Oyster Roasts. When the fall equinox begins until the later days of winter, the festivities all along Charleston include this briny delicacy. Rags, oyster knives, hot sauce, and warm clothes required.

Magnolia Blooms. The dinner-plate sized blossoms gently glide through the breezes to open windows and Southern verandas with their citrusy sweetness.

Wisteria, Jasmine, Honeysuckle and Gardenias. All promise that summer is near. It's hard to leave a shady porch with a swing when they are blooming. All of these are absolutely intoxicating. I pull petals and vines to keep by my bedside, close to my pillow.

Horse Diapers, downtown Charleston. It happens.

Sweet Olive. Probably the least talked about but sweetest of all Southern scents. And the honeybees know it too!

And last but not least, that wonderful mélange of America's finest cuisine, a five-block vortex of hunger that slaps your face when you exit the parking garage downtown anywhere at dinner time.

With all of the accolades of recent years bestowed upon our Holy City, I wouldn't be a bit surprised if we added the title "Most Aromatic City" to our repertoire.

**Renae Brabham**
Writer and Author, *Piddlin in Dixie*

*The guided tour. A must-do while visiting Charleston. Photo by Martha Lawrence*

*Reflections of a Good Day. Photo by Delk Haigler*

# The Photographers

**MARGE AGIN** ▪ Photography has always been a passion for Marge. After obtaining a masters degree from UCLA in an unrelated major, she decided to change course and join the world of photography.

Her professional career began in Southern California. She worked as an event photographer, a photographic illustrator for a publishing company and a portrait photographer specializing in outdoor photography. She used every effort to always work toward the goal of being a fine arts photographer.

Today, Marge works exclusively in fine arts photography, and her travels have taken her around the world. Presently she resides in the Lowcountry of coastal South Carolina, finding the images and

lifestyle of this area fascinating. Her work is an art form that encompasses the use of digital camera equipment and computer capabilities. The finished work combines her photographic talent, artistic imagination and production techniques that are unique. Her third book, *What It Means To Be Here,*

*Palmetto Bluff, Bluffton, the Lowcountry and Beyond* published by Lydia Inglett Ltd. Publishing explores the are with striking visual imagery. ▪ **www.margeaginphotography.com**

**RINNE ALLEN** ▪ Rinne Allen is a photographer living in Athens, Georgia. Working in both color and black & white, she enjoys docu-

menting process as a way to show the effort that goes into creating things. Rinne spends most of her days collaborating with chefs, artisans, and designers to document their work and the process of creating it.

Rinne has a background in fine art, and works out of her studio in an old house in her hometown. Her family has a large garden, and she makes her light drawings here.

Rinne's work has been published in over 12 books and in national and international magazines, as well as shown in galleries and educational institutions. Rinne also has a regular column about harvests that runs with the *New York Times* magazine and focuses on the Southern region that she calls home. ▪ **www.rinneallen.com**

**MICHELLE BOLTON** ▪ Michelle Bolton moved to the Lowcountry three years ago from Pinehurst, North Carolina, where she owned a custom design-build firm for 21 years. "I've always been drawn to architecture," she says. Though Bolton has also done professional photography for more than 25 years—she trained under Eva Longoria's personal photographer—being able to do so full time in Charleston is particularly inspiring for this self-described free spirit. One of her biggest requests is for children's portraiture. The subjects' eyes are Bolton's favorite focal point. "I also like lifestyle portraits and capturing a child in candid movement," she says. In addition to architecture and families, Bolton also shoots outdoor weddings, events and pets—but not a day goes by that she doesn't find time to take in the beautiful local landscape. "I photograph a sunrise or sunset almost every day somewhere in the Lowcountry," Bolton admits. Book a photo walk downtown where Bolton usually "catches" a sunset.
▪ **www.michelleboltonphotography.com**

**SANDRA DIMKE** ▪ After spending almost 20 years in architectural photography in Connecticut, Sandy and her husband, Russ retired to the exceptionally beautiful area of Beaufort, South Carolina. She now concentrates on fine art photography with a slight edge towards

impressionism. A traveler at heart, her journeys around the world have created a portfolio of dramatic, colorful, yet inspiring images. Born and raised in Schenectady, NY, Sandy graduated from Nazareth College in Rochester and received her MBA in Marketing from the University at Albany (NY). In 2010-11 Sandy created an exhibit and book called *Hands Across The Lowcountry* for the Beaufort Three-Century project. In the Fall of 2015 she published *Cats of Beaufort*, a photo essay soft-cover book, as a fund-raiser for Tabby House Shelter in Beaufort.

Her art has received acceptances and ribbons in over a dozen juried shows. In the past 20 years she has judged numerous photo competitions throughout New England, South Carolina and North Carolina. In 2011, she received certification in Image Analysis from the Photographic Society of America. She has taught numerous photography and photo software classes. Sandy presently serves as Director of the International Club Print Competition for the

Photographic Society of America and as a member of the executive board of Beaufort Art Association. She continues her efforts to bring public awareness to photography as an art. ▪ **www.dimkephotoart.com**

**PAUL ANDREW DUNKER** ▪ Paul Andrew Dunker (b. 1983) is an award winning American fine art photographer, known for surreal landscape images that are presented as extremely limited, large-format prints. A native of Michigan, Paul has lived and traveled extensively throughout the United States and Europe. While living in Los Angeles, California, Paul got his start doing lifestyle and event photography for

fashion and PR companies. His editorial work has been published in the *Los Angeles Times, US Magazine, Lucky Magazine,* and more; his creative works have been featured in magazines, books, and galleries around the world.

Upon moving to Charleston, South Carolina in the summer of 2013, Paul made the decision to leave the world of commercial photography, and to pursue his passion for fine art. Inspired by the vast beauty and raw power of the sea, much of Paul's work explores the relationship between land, sea, and sky. His ongoing series STRAND and ADRIFT display a consistency of vision and technique, and yet reflect the unique features of each landscape he visits. By employing specialized filters, long single exposures, he captures the movement of water and clouds. Each image is a visual meditation, inviting the viewer to leave the noise of modern life and to enter a world of calm and beauty.

In the fall of 2015, Paul moved to the French countryside, where he continues to create new work. ▪ **www.paulandrewdunker.com**

**JANET GARRITY** ▪ Author and photographer Janet Garrity resides in Beaufort, South Carolina, where she found inspiration to publish the first ever book about the South Carolina Sea Islands' fish camps. The book, *Goin' Down the River—Fish Camps of the Sea Islands*, is full of dramatic photos and clever writings that depict the tradition of "goin' down the river," a unique slice of Lowcountry history.

Janet has been in love with photography since picking up a camera when she was eight years old. Before moving to the Lowcountry, she lived

in Ithaca, NY, where she worked in marketing and advertising for 26 years. After moving to Beaufort in 2008, Janet dedicated herself to photography when a friend gave her the inspiration and determination to publish her photography work for the first time. Janet is currently working on her second book.
▪ **www.janetgarrity.com**

**DELK HAIGLER** ▪ Delk Haigler has honed his eye and his craft as a photographer in the Lowcountry of South Carolina. Delk specializes in long-exposure night shots that reveal detail and create an ambiance that heightens what we might normally see only during daylight hours. The result are photos that delight the viewer. ▪ **delkhaigler@yahoo.com**

**ERIC HORAN** ▪ Eric is a commercial and environmental photographer based in Beaufort, South Carolina. His lifelong passion photographing the natural beauty of the outdoors has provided an impressive portfolio. His pictures have a lyrical quality and speak to the viewer. "If not," he says, "then the image does not make the cut. If a picture works on me, then I'm betting it will for others." Over the years, Horan has won assignments from major magzines and corporations along with receiving notable awards. His work has been published in *Business Week, Fortune, Time, Newsweek, OUTSIDE, The New York Times Sunday Travel* and *Smithsonian* among other publishers including *Fodor's* and *National Geographic* books. His travel photography has also been recognized. When he helped a friend deliver a trawler to Florida, he captured a stunning, serendipitous image of a dolphin hitchhiking in the bow wake of the boat. This shot won a Carnegie Museum competition and later was selected for the cover of *Smithsonian*.

His just released, new book, *Beholding Nature* is a luxury coffee table book published by Lydia Inglett Publishing Ltd. ▪ **www.horanphoto.com**

**STEVEN HYATT** ▪ Steven's interest in photography emerged in his teenage years as an extension of a general desire to create. Years later, as a philosophy and religious studies major at the College of Charleston, he would often spend time "studying" in the Unitarian Church's incredibly unique and alive cemetery. He launched the Churches of Charleston Project which, 2 years later, became the Churches of America Project and has since expanded to include churches throughout the world. In addition to photographing churches Steven does a wide array of photography as personal or commercial endeavors ranging

Kim Graham Photography

from architecture to portraits of birds of prey to landscapes and abstract fine art photography. He also, has a printing business, Imaging Arts Printing, specializing in high quality printing of photographs or other artwork on canvas and various papers. ▪ **www.stevenhyatt.com**

**JONATHAN JACKSON** ▪ Jonathan Jackson is a landscape, fine art, and architectural photographer from Charleston, SC. A native of the Lowcountry, Jonathan's innate Charlestonian sense of preservation inspired him to begin photographing his incredible surroundings and he has since branched out to other cities, including New Orleans, Savannah, Beaufort and other coastal areas. Jonathan strives to capture the atmosphere of a place above all else, the raw beauty of a city's silent buildings and its surrounding environs. Jonathan has several series currently being released. Each series is available in large formats. Jonathan's work is also available on Metal Print and Stretched Canvas, both printed exclusively at Imaging Arts in Charleston, SC. All metal and canvas will be numbered in respective sizes, limited from 1 to 26 prints.

Jonathan's work has been featured in *Charleston City Paper, The Real Estate Studio on King St.*, Charleston Social Media Day, and various other Lowcountry venues. ▪ **www.jonathanjacksonphotography.com**

**TERRY KNIGHT** ▪ Terry Knight is the Owner / CEO of Flow Motion Productions. An alumnus of the University of Alabama, Terry is a producer, journalist and photographer.
▪ **tdurr@wyoming.com**

**MARTHA LAWRENCE** ▪ As a writer-photographer, Martha has researched, authored and illustrated numerous feature articles and publications including *Lightship Baskets of Nantucket* and *Scrimshaw the Whaler's Legacy*. A native of Boston and graduate of Simmons College, she continues her artistic endeavors in Vero Beach, Florida. ▪ **marthalawrence@gmail.com**

**KELLEY LUIKEY** ▪ Kelley Luikey is a South Carolina based photographer, teacher and Master Naturalist. As a lifelong outdoor enthusiast and adventure lover she is on (or under) the water with her camera as often as possible. Through her work, she hopes to inspire in others a love and appreciation of the beauty of the Lowcountry. Kelley resides in Beaufort with her husband Rich and their children Tristan and Arden. ▪ **www.naturemuseimagery.com**

**CHARLES MERRY** ▪ As a resident of Charleston, South Carolina, Charles Merry has been able to photograph many different people, parties, and landscapes. Starting out capturing the Charleston night life, Charles booked his first wedding shoot and fell in love. His passion lives in being able to capture moments that no one else may notice or remember. He wants the bride to come back a few weeks after the wedding, look at the photos, and genuinely be able to relive that moment in time. ▪ **www.charlesmerry.com**

**PAUL MULKEY** ▪ Paul Mulkey is a commercial photographer whose dynamic photographs of people, places and events are well known throughout the Lowcountry and nationally. His work appeared in 2015 Charleston Firefighters of South Carolina calendar to benefit the Charleston Animal Society. ▪ **www.paulmulkeyimages.com**

**RUSS PACE** ▪ Russ Pace is an award-winning photographer whose work has appeared in *Time, Newsweek, Sports Illustrated* and *Southern Living Wedding*. In January 2016, he retired from The Citadel, the Military College of South Carolina, after serving as director of photography for 30 years. At The Citadel, Pace photographed major college weekends from matriculation day to graduation, cadet life, athletic events, more than 700 military dress parades, and special events including the July 2007 Democratic Debate and President George W. Bush's post 9/11 speech. Special assignments took him to Capitol Hill, the Diamond Jubilee celebration of the Royal Edinburgh Tattoo in Scotland, the Royal Nova Scotia International Tattoo in Canada, the 2011 launch of the space shuttle Atlantis at Kennedy Space Center, the trading floor of the New York Stock Exchange and the top of the west tower of Charleston's Ravenel Bridge. In addition, Pace served as a Republican Party campaign photographer for Presidents Ronald Reagan and George H. Bush. He can be reached at ▪ **pacephoto@mac.com**

**KAREN M. PELUSO** ▪ Karen M. Peluso is a fine art photographer and poet. Her black and white images and select hand-painted prints have won numerous awards, and notably her image "Slaves' Cabins" won the 1st prize Rick Stevenson Memorial Award in Photography at the Beau-

fort Art Association's 2014 Spring Exhibit. Her art and poems have been published in the *Journal of NJ Poets; Connecticut Review; Kakalak* and *the new renaissance*, to name a few. Karen's first collection of poems, *The Mother-Face in the Mirror,* was awarded publication by distinguished poet Kwame Dawes as a winner of the 2006 SC Poetry Initiative Chapbook Series Contest. She then served as po-et-in-residence at Magnolia Plantation & Gardens

in Charleston in 2008. *Magnolia Plantation: A Journey,* a book of plantation experience poems and infrared photographs, was published later that year. The infrared images selected for *Charleston Salt and Iron* were two that she produced during her time at Magnolia. Karen lives in Beaufort, South Carolina with her husband Clinton B. Campbell, "The Leftover Gourmet." ▪ **www.karenmpelusophotography.com**

**TIM SAYER** ▪ With the town of Southern Pines in the sandhills of North Carolina serving as his home-base, Tim Sayer has been documenting the lives and businesses of clients throughout the East Coast for the past twelve years. Tim established Sayer Photography, a studio committed to providing an exciting option for high-end portraiture and innovative wedding photography.

Constantly striving to think outside of the box, Tim melds time-tested classic techniques with a fresh and innovative style that avoids trends and clichés or the dreaded canvas backdrop look. Whether

shooting in his studio or on location, he prides himself on finding unique ways to tell his clients stories, usually trying to tie in the relationships that his subjects share with the people and environments surrounding them. More than simply capturing a single moment in time, his images tell stories, each as unique and varied as the subjects they portray. Tim is the winner of the

2010 Wedding and Portrait Society Photographer of the Year Award. ▪ **www.sayerphotography.com**

**ELIZABETH SHER** ▪ Elizabeth is an editorial, travel and commercial photographer specializing in portraits and sporting lifestyle images. A native of South Carolina, she is currently based between St Helena Island, SC and Saluda, NC. Additional images, awards and clients can be seen on her website. She is

currently working on her new book. ▪ **www. elizabethsher.com**

**ROBBIE SILVER** ▪ As a lifelong resident in the Charleston area, Robbie learned to appreciate the interesting views that saturate the Lowcountry

area of South Carolina. Growing up in Mt. Pleasant, he developed an interest in art from an early age and always looked for outlets for this creative need. It took until 2004 before he really got interested in photography and his friends had to push him to get started. I bought my first SLR in 2006 and began shooting, training, reading and study-

ing everything he could find about photography. Finally, having enough of the corporate grind, Robbie left his job to pursue photography full time in 2008. ▪ **www.robbiesilver.com**

**TRIPP SMITH** ▪ Native to South Carolina and raised in the Charleston Lowcountry, as a boy Tripp Smith developed an eye for the play of light on the varied landscapes of marsh, creek and sea. After studying photography at the University of South Carolina and earning a Bachelor's degree in Media Arts, Tripp returned to Charleston and began to hone his talents as an apprentice alongside noted local photographers. Within a few years Tripp had developed a freelance career of his own and by 1998 Tripp began shooting full-time, crafting expressive and powerful images for architects, interior designers, and developers, as well as fine art B&W images for art galleries. He is a rugged naturalist, a defender of places untouched and unpolluted. "A good photographer concentrates on a certain subject that inspires them."

Tripp's deep love for art photography reflects notable artistic influences, his mother Charleston artist Betty Anglin Smith.

He is particularly adept at capturing the peace and ephemeral tranquility to be found throughout the barrier islands.

▪ **www.trippsmithphotography.com**

**AMELIA WEAVER** ▪ Amelia Weaver is originally from Columbus,

Ohio but has called Charleston home for the last decade. She earned a BFA in interior design from the Art Institute of Charleston. It is her fine art degree that helped define her eye with the camera. Line, shape, color, and composition are all things translatable in photography. It is the soul of the moments she finds most interesting. The human condition is in every photo, even if it is simply where they were. That is the common thread in all of her work. She is the owner of Amelia.E.Images and can rarely be seen without a camera in her hand.

▪ **ameliaeimages@gmail.com**

**LIBBY WILLIAMS** ▪ With a passion for a good story and all things photography, photographer Libby Williams realized early on that her

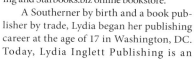

calling would be on the visual side of the storytelling game. Growing up around the shores of South Carolina, she would develop a love early on of the people, places and things that make this her home. Lately, Libby spends her time quietly documenting everything around

her, forever hoping to capture the essence of the simple and complex nature of everyday life. ▪ **www. libbywilliamsphotographs.com**

**ABOUT THE PUBLISHER** ▪ Lydia Inglett is CEO and Publisher of Lydia Inglett Publishing and Starbooks.biz online bookstore.

A Southerner by birth and a book publisher by trade, Lydia began her publishing career at the age of 17 in Washington, DC.

Today, Lydia Inglett Publishing is an award-winning, international publisher known for publishing lush, beautiful books on topics ranging from the Lowcountry to Paris and beyond.

She developed the unique business model for her company through years in traditional publishing. Her passion for beautiful books remains high in today's culture of electronic information.

Her publishing company has won numerous Benjamin Franklin Awards for excellence in publishing, USA Book Awards, and most recently the Independent Publisher Best Regional Non-Fiction Award.